RESUMES
FOR
HIGH SCHOOL
GRADUATES

VGM Professional Resumes Series

RESUMES
FOR
HIGH SCHOOL
GRADUATES

The Editors of
VGM Career Horizons

Second Edition

VGM Career Horizons
NTC/Contemporary Publishing Group

Library of Congress Cataloging-in-Publication Data

Resumes for high school graduates / the editors of VGM Career Horizons. —
2nd ed.
      p.   cm. — (VGM professional resumes series)
   ISBN 0-8442-1746-8
    1. Résumés (Employment).   2. High school graduates—Employment—
United States.   I. Series.
   HF5383.R438   1999
   808′.06665—DC21   98-36001
                                          CIP

ACKNOWLEDGMENT

We would like to acknowledge the assistance of Kathy Siebel
in compiling and editing this book.

Published by VGM Career Horizons
A division of NTC/Contemporary Publishing Group, Inc.
4255 West Touhy Avenue, Lincolnwood (Chicago), Illinois 60646-1975 U.S.A.
Copyright © 1999 by NTC/Contemporary Publishing Group, Inc.
Printed in the United States of America
International Standard Book Number: 0-8442-1746-8

99 00 01 02 03 04 VP 19 18 17 16 15 14 13 12 11 10 9 8 7 6 5 4 3 2 1

CONTENTS

Introduction

Your resume is your first impression on a prospective employer. Though you may be articulate, intelligent, and charming in person, a poor resume may prevent you from ever having the opportunity to demonstrate your interpersonal skills, because a poor resume may prevent you from ever being called for an interview. While few people have ever been hired solely on the basis of their resume, a well-written, well-organized resume can go a long way toward helping you land an interview. Your resume's main purpose is to get you that interview. The rest is up to you and the employer. If you both feel that you are right for the job and the job is right for you, chances are you will be hired.

A resume must catch the reader's attention yet still be easy to read and to the point. Resume styles have changed over the years. Today, brief and focused resumes are preferred. No longer do employers have the patience, or the time, to review several pages of solid type. A resume should be only one page long, if possible, and never more than two pages. Time is a precious commodity in today's business world and the resume that is concise and straightforward will usually be the one that gets noticed

Let's not make the mistake, though, of assuming that writing a brief resume means that you can take less care in preparing it. A successful resume takes time and thought, and if you are willing to make the effort, the rewards are well worth it. Think of your resume as a sales tool with the product being you. You want to sell yourself to a prospective employer. This book is designed to help you prepare a resume that will help you further your career—to land that next job, or first job, or to return to the work force after years of absence. So, read on. Make the effort and reap the rewards that a strong resume can being to your career. Let's get to it!

Chapter One

THE ELEMENTS OF A GOOD RESUME

A winning resume is made of the elements that employers are most interested in seeing when reviewing a job applicant. These basic elements are the essential ingredients of a successful resume and become the actual sections of your resume. The following is a list of elements that may be used in a resume. Some are essential; some are optional. We will be discussing these in this chapter in order to give you a better understanding of each element's role in the makeup of your resume:

1. Heading
2. Objective
3. Work Experience
4. Education
5. Honors
6. Activities
7. Certificates and Licenses
8. Professional Memberships
9. Special Skills
10. Personal Information
11. References

The first step in preparing your resume is to gather together information about yourself and your past accomplishments. Later you will refine this information, rewrite it in the most effective language, and organize it into the most attractive layout. First, let's take a look at each of these important elements individually.

Heading

The heading may seem to be a simple enough element in your resume, but be careful not to take it lightly. The heading should be placed at the top of your resume and should include your name, home address, and telephone numbers. If you can take calls at your current place of business, include your business number, since most employers will attempt to contact you during the business day. If this is not possible, or if you can afford it, purchase an answering machine that allows you to retrieve your messages while you are away from home. This way you can make sure you don't miss important phone calls. Always include your phone number on your resume. It is crucial that when prospective employers need to have immediate contact with you, they can.

Objective

When seeking a particular career path, it is important to list a job objective on your resume. This statement helps employers know the direction that you see yourself heading, so that they can determine whether your goals are in line with the position available. The objective is normally one sentence long and describes your employment goals clearly and concisely. See the sample resumes in this book for examples of objective statements.

The job objective will vary depending on the type of person you are, the field you are in, and the type of goals you have. It can be either specific or general, but it should always be to the point.

In some cases, this element is not necessary, but usually it is a good idea to include your objective. It gives your possible future employer an idea of where you are coming from and where you want to go.

The objective statement is better left out, however, if you are uncertain of the exact title of the job you seek. In such a case, the inclusion of an overly specific objective statement could result in your not being considered for a variety of acceptable positions; you should be sure to incorporate this information in your cover letter, instead.

Work Experience

This element is arguably the most important of them all. It will provide the central focus of your resume, so it is necessary that this section be as complete as possible. Only by examining your work experience in depth can you get to the heart of your accomplishments and present them in a way that demonstrates the strength of your qualifications. Of course, someone just out of school will have less work experience than someone who has been working for a number of years, but the amount of information isn't the most important thing—rather, how it is presented and how it highlights you as a person and as a worker will be what counts.

As you work on this section of your resume, be aware of the need for accuracy. You'll want to include all necessary information about each of your jobs, including job title, dates, employer, city, state, responsibilities, special projects, and accomplishments. Be sure to only list company accomplishments for which you were directly responsible. If you haven't participated in any special projects, that's all right—this area may not be relevant to certain jobs.

The most common way to list your work experience is in *reverse chronological order*. In other words, start with your most recent job and work your way backwards. This way your prospective employer sees your current (and often most important) job before seeing your past jobs. Your most recent position, if the most important, should also be the one that includes the most information, as compared to your previous positions. If you are just out of school, show your summer employment and part-time work, though in this case your education will most likely be more important than your work experience.

The following worksheets will help you gather information about your past jobs.

WORK EXPERIENCE
Job One:

Job Title _Part time_ _____

Dates _____

Employer _____

City, State _____

Major Duties _____

_____

_____

_____

_____

_____

_____

_____

Special Projects _____

_____

_____

_____

Accomplishments _____

_____

_____

_____

_____

_____

_____

_____

Job Four:

Job Title _____

Dates _____

Employer _____

City, State _____

Major Duties _____

_____

_____

_____

_____

_____

_____

Special Projects _____

_____

_____

_____

Accomplishments_____

_____

_____

_____

_____

_____

_____

_____

Education

Education is the second most important element of a resume. Your educational background is often a deciding factor in an employer's decision to hire you. Be sure to stress your accomplishments in school with the same finesse that you stressed your accomplishments at work. If you are looking for your first job, your education will be your greatest asset, since your work experience will most likely be minimal. In this case, the education section becomes the most important. You will want to be sure to include any degrees or certificates you received, your major area of concentration, any honors, and any relevant activities. Again, be sure to list your most recent schooling first. If you have completed graduate-level work, begin with that and work in reverse chronological order through your undergraduate education. If you have completed an undergraduate degree, you may choose whether to list your high school experience or not. This should be done only if your high school grade-point average was well above average.

The following worksheets will help you gather information for this section of your resume. Also included are supplemental worksheets for honors and for activities. Sometimes honors and activities are listed in a section separate from education, most often near the end of the resume.

EDUCATION

School _____

Major or Area of Concentration _____

Degree _____

Date _____

School _____

Major or Area of Concentration _____

Degree _____

Date _____

Honors

Here, you should list any awards, honors, or memberships in honorary societies that you have received. Usually these are of an academic nature, but they can also be for special achievement in sports, clubs, or other school activities. Always be sure to include the name of the organization honoring you and the date(s) received. Use the worksheet below to help gather your honors information.

HONORS

Honor: _____

Awarding Organization: _____

Date(s): _____

Honor: _____

Awarding Organization: _____

Date(s): _____

Honor: _____

Awarding Organization: _____

Date(s): _____

Honor: _____

Awarding Organization: _____

Date(s): _____

Activities

You may have been active in different organizations or clubs during your years at school; often an employer will look at such involvement as evidence of initiative and dedication. Your ability to take an active role, and even a leadership role, in a group should be included on your resume. Use the worksheet provided to list your activities and accomplishments in this area. In general, you should exclude any organization the name of which indicates the race, creed, sex, age, marital status, color, or nation of origin of its members.

ACTIVITIES

Organization/Activity: _____

Accomplishments: _____

_____

_____

Organization/Activity: _____

Accomplishments: _____

_____

_____

Organization/Activity: _____

Accomplishments: _____

_____

_____

Organization/Activity: _____

Accomplishments: _____

_____

_____

As your work experience increases through the years, your school activities and honors will play less of a role in your resume, and eventually you will most likely only list your degree and any major honors you received. This is due to the fact that, as time goes by, your job performance becomes the most important element in your resume. Through time, your resume should change to reflect this.

Certificates and Licenses

The next potential element of your resume is certificates and licenses. You should list these if the job you are seeking requires them and you, of course, have acquired them. If you have applied for a license, but have not yet received it, use the phrase "application pending."

License requirements vary by state. If you have moved or you are planning to move to another state, be sure to check with the appropriate board or licensing agency in the state in which you are applying for work to be sure that you are aware of all licensing requirements.

Always be sure that all of the information you list is completely accurate. Locate copies of your licenses and certificates and check the exact date and name of the accrediting agency. Use the following worksheet to list your licenses and certificates.

CERTIFICATES AND LICENSES

Name of License: _____

Licensing Agency: _____

Date Issued: _____

Name of License: _____

Licensing Agency: _____

Date Issued: _____

Name of License: _____

Licensing Agency: _____

Date Issued: _____

Professional Memberships

Another potential element in your resume is a section listing professional memberships. Use this section to list involvement in professional associations, unions, and similar organizations. It is to your advantage to list any professional memberships that pertain to the job you are seeking. Be sure to include the dates of your involvement and whether you took part in any special activities or held any offices within the organization. Use the following worksheet to gather your information.

PROFESSIONAL MEMBERSHIPS

Name of Organization: _____

Offices Held: _____

Activities: _____

Date(s): _____

Name of Organization: _____

Offices Held: _____

Activities: _____

Date(s): _____

Name of Organization: _____

Offices Held: _____

Activities: _____

Date(s): _____

Name of Organization: _____

Offices Held: _____

Activities: _____

Date(s): _____

Special Skills

This section of your resume is set aside for mentioning any special abilities you have that could relate to the job you are seeking. This is the part of your resume where you have the opportunity to demonstrate certain talents and experiences that are not necessarily a part of your educational or work experience. Common examples include fluency in a foreign language, or knowledge of a particular computer application.

Special skills can encompass a wide range of your talents—remember to be sure that whatever skills you list relate to the type of work you are looking for.

Personal Information

Some people include "Personal" information on their resumes. This is not generally recommended, but you might wish to include it if you think that something in your personal life, such as a hobby or talent, has some bearing on the position you are seeking. This type of information is often referred to at the beginning of an interview, when it is used as an "ice breaker." Of course, personal information regarding age, marital status, race, religion, or sexual preference should never appear on any resume.

References

References are not usually listed on the resume, but a prospective employer needs to know that you have references who may be contacted if necessary. All that is necessary to include in your resume regarding references is a sentence at the bottom stating, "References are available upon request." If a prospective employer requests a list of references, be sure to have one ready. Also, check with whomever you list to see if it is all right for you to use them as a reference. Forewarn them that they may receive a call regarding a reference for you. This way they can be prepared to give you the best reference possible.

Chapter Two

WRITING YOUR RESUME

*N*ow that you have gathered together all of the information for each of the sections of your resume, it's time to write out each section in a way that will get the attention of whoever is reviewing it. The type of language you use in your resume will affect its success. You want to take the information you have gathered and translate it into a language that will cause a potential employer to sit up and take notice.

Resume writing is not like expository writing or creative writing. It embodies a functional, direct writing style and focuses on the use of action words. By using action words in your writing, you more effectively stress past accomplishments. Action words help demonstrate your initiative and highlight your talents. Always use verbs that show strength and reflect the qualities of a "doer." By using action words, you characterize yourself as a person who takes action, and this will impress potential employers.

The following is a list of verbs commonly used in resume writing. Use this list to choose the action words that can help your resume become a strong one:

administered	introduced
advised	invented
analyzed	maintained
arranged	managed
assembled	met with
assumed responsibility	motivated
billed	negotiated
built	operated
carried out	orchestrated
channeled	ordered
collected	organized
communicated	oversaw
compiled	performed
completed	planned
conducted	prepared
contacted	presented
contracted	produced
coordinated	programmed
counseled	published
created	purchased
cut	recommended
designed	recorded
determined	reduced
developed	referred
directed	represented
dispatched	researched
distributed	reviewed
documented	saved
edited	screened
established	served as
expanded	served on
functioned as	sold
gathered	suggested
handled	supervised
hired	taught
implemented	tested
improved	trained
inspected	typed
interviewed	wrote

Now take a look at the information you put down on the work experience worksheets. Take that information and rewrite it in paragraph form, using verbs to highlight your actions and accomplishments. Let's look at an example, remembering that what matters here is the writing style, and not the particular job responsibilities given in our sample.

WORK EXPERIENCE
Regional Sales Manager

Manager of sales representatives from seven states. Responsible for twelve food chain accounts in the East. In charge of directing the sales force in planned selling toward specific goals. Supervisor and trainer of new sales representatives. Consulting for customers in the areas of inventory management and quality control.

Special Projects: Coordinator and sponsor of annual food industry sales seminar.

Accomplishments: Monthly regional volume went up 25 percent during my tenure while, at the same time, a proper sales/cost ratio was maintained. Customer/company relations improved significantly.

Below is the rewritten version of this information, using action words. Notice how much stronger it sounds.

WORK EXPERIENCE
Regional Sales Manager

Managed sales representatives from seven states. Handled twelve food chain accounts in the eastern United States. Directed the sales force in planned selling towards specific goals. Supervised and trained new sales representatives. Consulted for customers in the areas of inventory management and quality control. Coordinated and sponsored the annual Food Industry Seminar. Increased monthly regional volume 25 percent and helped to improve customer/company relations during my tenure.

Another way of constructing the work experience section is by using actual job descriptions. Job descriptions are rarely written using the proper resume language, but they do include all the information necessary to create this section of your resume. Take the description of one of the jobs your are including on your resume (if you have access to it), and turn it into an action-oriented paragraph. Below is an example of a job description followed by a version of the same description written using action words. Again, pay attention to the style of writing, as the details of your own work experience will be unique.

PUBLIC ADMINISTRATOR I

Responsibilities: Coordinate and direct public services to meet the needs of the nation, state, or community. Analyze problems; work with special committees and public agencies; recommend solutions to governing bodies.

Aptitudes and Skills: Ability to relate to and communicate with people; solve complex problems through analysis; plan, organize, and implement policies and programs. Knowledge of political systems; financial management; personnel administration; program evaluation; organizational theory.

WORK EXPERIENCE
Public Administrator I

Wrote pamphlets and conducted discussion groups to inform citizens of legislative processes and consumer issues. Organized and supervised 25 interviewers. Trained interviewers in effective communication skills.

Now that you have learned how to word your resume, you are ready for the next step in your quest for a winning resume: assembly and layout.

Chapter Three

ASSEMBLY AND LAYOUT

*A*t this point, you've gathered all the necessary information for your resume, and you've rewritten it using the language necessary to impress potential employers. Your next step is to assemble these elements in a logical order and then to lay them out on the page neatly and attractively in order to achieve the desired effect: getting that interview.

Assembly

The order of the elements in a resume makes a difference in its overall effect. Obviously, you would not want to put your name and address in the middle of the resume or your special skills section at the top. You want to put the elements in an order that stresses your most important achievements, not the less pertinent information. For example, if you recently graduated from school and have no full-time work experience, you will want to list your education before you list any part-time jobs you may have held during school. On the other hand, if you have been gainfully employed for several years and currently hold an important position in your company, you will want to list your work experience ahead of your education, which has become less pertinent with time.

There are some elements that are always included in your resume and some that are optional. Following is a list of essential and optional elements:

Essential	*Optional*
Name	Job Objective
Address	Honors
Phone Number	Special Skills
Work Experience	Professional Memberships
Education	Activities
References Phrase	Certificates and Licenses
	Personal Information

Your choice of optional sections depends on your own background and employment needs. Always use information that will put you and your abilities in a favorable light. If your honors are impressive, then be sure to include them in your resume. If your activities in school demonstrate particular talents necessary for the job you are seeking, then allow space for a section on activities. Each resume is unique, just as each person is unique.

Types of Resumes

So far, our discussion about resumes has involved the most common type—the *reverse chronological* resume, in which your most recent job is listed first and so on. This is the type of resume usually preferred by human resources directors, and it is the one most frequently used. However, in some cases this style of presentation is not the most effective way to highlight your skills and accomplishments.

For someone reentering the work force after many years or someone looking to change career fields, the *functional resume* may work best. This type of resume focuses more on achievement and less on the sequence of your work history. In the functional resume, your experience is presented by what you have accomplished and the skills you have developed in your past work.

A functional resume can be assembled from the same information you collected for your chronological resume. The main difference lies in how you organize this information. Essentially, the work experience section becomes two sections, with your job duties and accomplishments comprising one section and your employer's name, city, state, your position, and the dates employed making up another section. The first section is placed near the top of the resume, just below the job objective section, and can be called *Accomplishments* or *Achievements*. The second section, containing the bare essentials of your employment history, should come after the accomplishments section and can be titled *Work Experience* or *Employment History*. The other sections of your resume remain the same. The work experience section is the only one affected in the functional resume. By placing the section that focuses on your achievements first, you thereby draw attention to these achievements. This puts less emphasis on who you worked for and more emphasis on what you did and what you are capable of doing.

For someone changing careers, emphasis on skills and achievements is essential. The identities of previous employers, which may be unrelated to one's new job field, need to be downplayed. The functional resume accomplishes this task. For someone reentering the work force after many years, a functional resume is the obvious choice. If you lack full-time work experience, you will need to draw attention away from this fact and instead focus on your skills and abilities gained possibly through volunteer activities or part-time work. Education may also play a more important role in this resume.

Which type of resume is right for you will depend on your own personal circumstances. It may be helpful to create a chronological *and* a functional resume and then compare the two to find out which is more suitable. The sample resumes found in this book include both chronological and functional resumes. Use these resumes as guides to help you decide on the content and appearance of your own resume.

Layout

Once you have decided which elements to include in your resume and you have arranged them in an order that makes sense and emphasizes your achievements and abilities, then it is time to work on the physical layout of your resume.

There is no single appropriate layout that applies to every resume, but there are a few basic rules to follow in putting your resume on paper:

1. Leave a comfortable margin on the sides, top, and bottom of the page (usually 1 to 1½ inches).

2. Use appropriate spacing between the sections (usually 2 to 3 line spaces are adequate).

3. Be consistent in the *type* of headings you use for the different sections of your resume. For example, if you capitalize the heading EMPLOYMENT HISTORY, don't use initial capitals and underlining for a heading of equal importance, such as Education.

4. Always try to fit your resume onto one page. If you are having trouble fitting all your information onto one page, perhaps you are trying to say too much. Try to edit out any repetitive or unnecessary information or possibly shorten descriptions of earlier jobs. Be ruthless. Maybe you've included too many optional sections.

CHRONOLOGICAL RESUME

Alicia Bernard
3180 SE Pelton Avenue
Rumford, Maine 04276   (207) 555-0590

Objective   Secretarial or receptionist position

Education

1995 - present   Mountain Valley High School, Hancock Street, Rumford, ME

Relevant courses: Keyboarding, Office Systems, Personal Finance, Russian, currently enrolled in Shorthand.

Spring 1994   Anna Falaci's Charm School, Mountain Road, Oxford, ME

Work Experience

7/98-8/98   Landscaping, Crest Landscaping Services
My responsibilities included pruning, trimming, weeding, and mowing for a variety of business and individual clients.

6/97-8/97   Assistant, Duckworth Boats
My duties included working with the public, serving as receptionist, typing, answering telephones, bookkeeping, filing, receiving and sending shipments. Also washed and detailed boats and assisted at boat shows.

6/96-9/96   Volunteer, Animal Services, Oxford County Animal Control
I was responsible for feeding and bathing animals in the animal control shelter, showing pets to prospective owners, and answering telephones.

1992-present   Child Care Provider, Various Individuals
Provide care to children ages six weeks to nine years, from one to three children at a time.

1992 - 1995   General Assistant, Webb's K.E. Carlson Co.
Duties included typing, filing, data entry, cleaning, and running errands.

Skills   Computer keyboarding, communications and telephone skills, filing, general office work.

References   Available on request

FUNCTIONAL RESUME

DONNA MURAR
810 Fifth Street N.
Canton, South Dakota 57013
(605) 555-9530

Objective

Entry-level position with an international corporation where my bilingual skills may make a contribution to the organization.

Education

Canton High School, 112 Elder Avenue E., Canton, SD 57013
Graduation Date: 1999

Attended school in Romania during 1997-1998 school year.

Training

Computer applications experience: Word on IBM and Mac;
Lotus 1-2-3, dBase, and Harvard Graphics on IBM.

Computer word processing speed: 70 w.p.m.

Office systems course covered bookkeeping, filing, telephone switchboards, personnel, and payroll.

Gregg shorthand speed: 115 w.p.m.

Fluent in Spanish; conversant in Romanian.

Work Experience

Attendance office assistant, Canton Senior High School, Sept. 1998-present.
Duties: answer telephones, assist students and faculty, prepare daily announcements list on computer, operate office machines, type and file.

Cashier, Kentucky Fried Chicken, June 1998-Sept. 1998.
Duties: Completed customer orders, entered sales in cash register, provided accurate change.

References

Available on request.

Don't let the idea of having to tell every detail about your life get in the way of producing a resume that is simple and straightforward. The more compact your resume, the easier it will be to read and the better an impression it will make for you.

In some cases, the resume will not fit on a single page, even after extensive editing. In such cases, the resume should be printed on two pages so as not to compromise clarity or appearance. Each page of a two-page resume should be marked clearly with your name and the page number, e.g., "Judith Ramirez, page 1 of 2." The pages should then be stapled together.

Try experimenting with various layouts until you find one that looks good to you. Always show your final layout to other people and ask them what they like or dislike about it, and what impresses them most about your resume. Make sure that is what you want most to emphasize. If it isn't, you may want to consider making changes in your layout until the necessary information is emphasized. Use the sample resumes in this book to get some ideas for laying out your resume.

Putting Your Resume in Print

Your resume should be typed or printed on good quality 8½" × 11" bond paper. You want to make as good an impression as possible with your resume; therefore, quality paper is a necessity. If you have access to a word processor with a good printer, or know of someone who does, make use of it. Typewritten resumes should only be used when there are no other options available.

After you have produced a clean original, you will want to make duplicate copies of it. Usually a copy shop is your best bet for producing copies without smudges or streaks. Make sure you have the copy shop use quality bond paper for all copies of your resume. Ask for a sample copy before they run your entire order. After copies are made, check each copy for cleanliness and clarity.

Another more costly option is to have your resume typeset and printed by a printer. This will provide the most attractive resume of all. If you anticipate needing a lot of copies of your resume, the cost of having it typeset may be justified.

Proofreading

After you have finished typing the master copy of your resume and before you go to have it copied or printed, you must thoroughly check it for typing and spelling errors. Have several people read it over just in case you may have missed an error. Misspelled words and typing mistakes will not make a good impression on a prospective employer, as they are a bad reflection on your writing ability and your attention to detail. With thorough and conscientious proofreading, these mistakes can be avoided.

The following are some rules of capitalization and punctuation that may come in handy when proofreading your resume:

Rules of Capitalization

- Capitalize proper nouns, such as names of schools, colleges, and universities, names of companies, and brand names of products.

- Capitalize major words in the names and titles of books, tests, and articles that appear in the body of your resume.

- Capitalize words in major section headings of your resume.

- Do not capitalize words just because they seem important.

- When in doubt, consult a manual of style such as *Words Into Type* (Prentice-Hall), or *The Chicago Manual of Style* (The University of Chicago Press). Your local library can help you locate these and other reference books.

Rules of Punctuation

- Use a comma to separate words in a series.

- Use a semicolon to separate series of words that already include commas within the series.

- Use a semicolon to separate independent clauses that are not joined by a conjunction.

- Use a period to end a sentence.

- Use a colon to show that the examples or details that follow expand or amplify the preceding phrase.

- Avoid the use of dashes.

- Avoid the use of brackets.

- If you use any punctuation in an unusual way in your resume, be consistent in its use.

- Whenever you are uncertain, consult a style manual.

Chapter Four

THE COVER LETTER

*O*nce your resume has been assembled, laid out, and printed to your satisfaction, the next and final step before distribution is to write your cover letter. Though there may be instances where you deliver your resume in person, most often you will be sending it through the mail. Resumes sent through the mail always need an accompanying letter that briefly introduces you and your resume. The purpose of the cover letter is to get a potential employer to read your resume, just as the purpose of your resume is to get that same potential employer to call you for an interview.

Like your resume, your cover letter should be clean, neat, and direct. A cover letter usually includes the following information:

1. Your name and address (unless it already appears on your personal letterhead).

2. The date.

3. The name and address of the person and company to whom you are sending your resume.

4. The salutation ("Dear Mr." or "Dear Ms." followed by the person's last name, or "To Whom It May Concern" if you are answering a blind ad).

5. An opening paragraph explaining why you are writing (in response to an ad, the result of a previous meeting, at the suggestion of someone you both know) and indicating that you are interested in whatever job is being offered.

6. One or two more paragraphs that tell why you want to work for the company and what qualifications and experience you can bring to that company.

7. A final paragraph that closes the letter and requests that you be contacted for an interview. You may mention here that your references are available upon request.

8. The closing ("Sincerely," or "Yours Truly," followed by your signature with your name typed under it).

Your cover letter, including all of the information above, should be no more than one page in length. The language used should be polite, businesslike, and to the point. Do not attempt to tell your life story in the cover letter. A long and cluttered letter will only serve to put off the reader. Remember, you only need to mention a few of your accomplishments and skills in the cover letter. The rest of your information is in your resume. Each and every achievement should not be mentioned twice. If your cover letter is a success, your resume will be read and all pertinent information reviewed by your prospective employer.

Producing the Cover Letter

Cover letters should always be typed individually, since they are always written to particular individuals and companies. Never use a form letter for your cover letter. Cover letters cannot be copied or reproduced like resumes. Each one should be as personal as possible. Of course, once you have written and rewritten your first cover letter to the point where you are satisfied with it, you certainly can use similar wording in subsequent letters.

After you have typed your cover letter on quality bond paper, be sure to proofread it as thoroughly as you did your resume. Again, spelling errors are a sure sign of carelessness, and you don't want that to be a part of your first impression on a prospective employer. Make sure to handle the letter and resume carefully to avoid any smudges, and then mail both your cover letter and resume in an appropriate sized envelope. Be sure to keep an accurate record of all the resumes you send out and the results of each mailing, either in a separate notebook or on individual 3×5" index cards.

Numerous sample cover letters appear at the end of the book. Use them as models for your own cover letter or to get an idea of how cover letters are put together. Remember, every one is unique and depends on the particular circumstances of the individual writing it and the job for which he or she is applying.

Now the job of writing your resume and cover letter is complete. About a week after mailing resumes and cover letters to potential employers, you will want to contact them by telephone. Confirm that your resume arrived, and ask whether an interview might be possible. Getting your foot in the door during this call is half the battle of a job search, and a strong resume and cover letter will help you immeasurably.

Chapter Five

SAMPLE RESUMES

This chapter contains dozens of sample resumes for people pursuing a wide variety of jobs and careers.

There are many different styles of resumes in terms of graphic layout and presentation of information. These samples also represent people with varying amounts of education and experience. Use these samples to model your own resume after. Choose one resume, or borrow elements from several different resumes to help you construct your own.

Andrew G. Meunier
6300 Beasley Road   Jackson, Mississippi 39225   601/555-7819

Personal Objective	Job with automotive repair or body shop
Experience	**Automotive Repair and Body Work**

*Assisted with complete exterior repair of six cars

*Assisted in engine repair and rebuild

*Detail painting on two vans

*Interior work on several vans

Home Maintenance

*Provided landscaping maintenance for apartment complex

*Interior and exterior painting of two homes

*Assisted with roofing of one new home and repair on another

*Minor carpentry work for apartment complex

Work History

Handyman   1997-present
Delta Apartments
2400 Albermarle Road
Jackson, MS 39213
Supervisor: Adrain Florio

Duties: landscape maintenance, carpentry, general repair.

Custodian   1996-1997
Alternative Junior High School
1900 N. State Street
Jackson, MS 39202
Supervisor: Johnson Ableman

Duties: basic janitorial work.

Skills & Activities   Sign language, drawing, and painting, member of Car Rally
Club of Jackson, Boy Scouts of America (Eagle Scout).

Education   Wingfield Senior High School
1985 Scanlon Drive
Jackson, MS
Diploma received June 1998

Courses: auto mechanics, wood shop, Spanish

References   Available on request

LaToya Cook

512 Lynn Road, Excelsior Springs, MO 64024
816/555-3225   or E-Mail: lacook@aol.com

Goal: A position involving writing and editing.

Experience: **Editor,** *The Easterly Breeze* (student newspaper)

~Wrote series on racial integration programs in Missouri high schools that won a state Junior Journalist award in 1996 from the Missouri Association of Newspaper Journalists. One article from the series was published in the MANJ newsletter.

~Write monthly column about student life and issues at East High School.

~Interview teachers and students for personality profile articles for publication in the student newspaper.

~Edit stories written by other students for spelling, grammar, and AP news style.

Reporter, *Encounters* (student yearbook)

~Wrote articles on sports for publication in yearbook.

~Wrote captions for photographs.

~Assisted staff photographers with taking group photographs.

Education: East High School
101 Richmond Street
Excelsior Springs, MO 64024
9/95 - 6/98
Current GPA: 3.75

Pertinent Courses: Journalism, Photography, Honors English (three years), Intro. to Law, American Government

References: Available on request

Shawana Udey   2354 S.E. Grand Avenue
                               Billings, Montana 59105
                               (406) 555-5835

Job Desired   Preschool or day care teaching assistant

Work Experience

6/96-present   Childcare Provider, Faubian Elementary School
                    3039 N.E. Sierra Boulevard
                    Billings, MT 59102
                    (406) 555-5085
                    Supervisor: Nancy Toppila

                    Duties: Provide childcare during adult education parenting classes.

6/95-present   Volunteer, St. Vincent's Hospital
                    2915 Twelfth Avenue
                    Billings, MT 59101
                    (406) 254-2333
                    Supervisor: Jamilla de Corazon, R.N.

                    Duties: Work as candy striper, providing reading material, reading
                    aloud, visiting with patients, and assisting nurses.

Education

9/94-6/98   Skyview High School, 1775 High Sierra Boulevard, Billings, MT

                    Relevant Coursework:
                    One year each: Child Development, Teacher Assistant,
                    Home Economics and Nutrition, Health and Fitness

Related Skills *CPR and basic emergency first aid certification
                    *Training in baby-sitting from Yellowstone County Red Cross
                    *Completion of infant care courses at St. Vincent's Hospital

                    References on Request

Estrella Angelino
2240 W. Yucca Street
Santa Fe, New Mexico 87538
(505) 555-5121

Objective   Finding a challenging part-time job in sales and customer service with opportunity for future advancement.

Relevant
Coursework

Typing I & II	Office Systems and Procedures
English I, II, & III	Computer Applications I & II
Finance and Accounting I & II	Computer Accounting

Education   Capitol High School, Santa Fe
Diploma Awarded June 1998

Work
Experience   **Square Pan Pizza,** Paseo del Sol, Santa Fe
(Hired April 1997; store closed December 1997)

My responsibilities included greeting customers, taking orders, handling cash, operating the register, answering telephones, cooking, cleaning, and assisting with closing.

The Bite of Santa Fe
(Volunteer in 1996-1998)

Served as volunteer for the city's annual weekend celebration of food and music in downtown Santa Fe. Duties included working with the public, taking orders, handling cash, and serving ice cream and soft drinks.

St. Vincent de Paul, Santa Fe
(Volunteer since 1997)

Worked as a volunteer helping serve food and distribute clothing and supplies to people in need.

REFERENCES AVAILABLE

Alexander Hyde Branch III
Rural Route 7, Box 43B
Geneva, Nebraska 68361
(402) 555-2822

Job Desired
Bank teller or bank clerk with opportunities for utilizing my education in finance and accounting.

Education

9/96 - present
Geneva North High School
Rural Route 7, Box 23A
Geneva, Nebraska 68361

Achievements
Completed series of accounting courses that involved recording and analyzing financial transactions, developing financial plans, and preparing financial statements.

Learned computer-assisted accounting using two different software programs: AAACPAC Plus and Lotus 1-2-3.

Participated in class-run simulated business as financial manager. Developed business plan and worked with marketing manager to carry out business objectives.

Participated in career visitations to a variety of financial institutions.

Activities
Vice-President, Future Business Leaders of America
Member, DECA (marketing club)
Reporter on student newspaper
Treasurer, National Honor Society

Work History

5/98 - present
Burger King
366 N.W. Frontage
Geneva, Nebraska 68361
Supervisor: Bobbie Mahew

Duties: As a line cashier, I greet my customers, take orders, prepare food, handle cash, and balance receipts against sales at the end of my shift. I have never been late to work or missed a day. Chosen as Cashier of the Month, July 1998.

References
Available upon request.

PATRICIA FINLEY

351 N. 22nd ~ Las Vegas, Nevada 89102 ~ (702) 555-1377

JOB GOALS
Entry-level position in bank or bookkeeping firm.

EDUCATION
Clark Senior High School, 4291 Pennwood Avenue, Las Vegas
Expected graduation date: 1999

Courses of Study:
Math (three years), Accounting II, Computer Systems; currently enrolled in Japanese I, Advanced Algebra, and serving as a Teacher Assistant.

EXPERIENCE
Experienced with payroll reports and bookkeeping. Studied federal and state payroll tax guidelines and prepared quarterly reports. Assumed responsibility for three small-business accounts, maintaining income and expense ledgers and providing monthly statements.

Experienced with general ledger accounting on ACCPAC software.

Served as Treasurer for the marketing club and was responsible for maintaining the sales and expense records for the Student Store.

WORK HISTORY
Finley & Associates, CPAs, Las Vegas. Summers 1996-present.

ACTIVITIES
Portfolio Club: Earned 27 percent on investments made in mock stock-market investment program for business students.

Marketing Club Treasurer; elected from among 82 student members; attended regional convention in Santa Fe, New Mexico, to represent our chapter's school store innovations.

National Honor Society/ School Honor Roll

Spanish Club. Helped plan club-sponsored field trips and a Spanish banquet to raise funds for a trip to Mexico.

REFERENCES
Available on request

Marshall L. Floyd

2825 Evans Avenue, Suncook, New Hampshire 03275
(212) 555-9941

Professional Goal   Summer assistant to state legislator

Education

1995-present   Pembroke Academy, Suncook, New Hampshire
                 Expected graduation date: 1999

1993-1994   Exeter School for Boys, Exeter, New Hampshire

Relevant Courses   *American Government
                         *Business Law
                         *Western Civilization
                         *World History
                         *Sociology

Work Experience

June- August 1998   Briscoe and Havering, Attorneys at Law, Manchester, New Hampshire

                      Duties: Worked with attorneys and legal assistants to gather
                      documentation needed for litigation proceedings. Assisted with research,
                      maintained legal library records, and obtained necessary materials from
                      central law library at the college.

Skills   *Experienced with computers (Word Perfect, dBase on IBM)
                      *Good research skills
                      *Typing, 45 w.p.m.

Activities   *Went to state competition as a member of Model United Nations (Greece)
                      *Member of Future Business Leaders of America
                      *Served as Outdoor School Junior Counselor for three sessions
                      *Coached Junior Soccer for the Boys & Girls Club of Merrimack County

References   Available on request

MIKE BOYLE

288 Palisade Avenue ~ Jersey City, New Jersey 07306 ~ 201-555-2938

JOB DESIRED Apprentice mechanic with automotive repair company with opportunity to train as auto mechanic.

EDUCATION Dickinson High School, Jersey City, 1996 to present
Hudson Regional Junior-Senior High School, Highlands, NJ 1994-1996

SKILLS Mechanically inclined with skills ranging from basic auto mechanics to very technical electrical diagnostics.

Experienced with engine overhaul, suspension, brakes, fuel, power train, and motor detailing.

Some auto-body repair experience.

WORK EXPERIENCE Dickinson High School Auto Shop, 1997-present

Duties: Tune-ups, oil changes, general check-up and trouble shooting in student-run auto mechanics shop. Diagnose and repair mechanical problems on cars, trucks, and vans.

East Jersey Radiator, 1997-presnt

Duties: Cleaning and testing radiators, installing replacement radiators, and motor detailing. Shop services both foreign and domestic cars. Assisted with stock warehouse.

Northern Landscape Maintenance, 1996-1997

Duties: Planting, mowing, pruning, and hedging for three apartment complexes and four office complexes. Responsible for maintaining nursery inventory.

REFERENCES Available upon request.

ARLENE HOSKA

2833 Kennedy Boulevard   Telephone: (201) 555-5198
Jersey City, New Jersey 07305   Fax: (201) 555-9877

OBJECTIVE   To obtain a position as receptionist for a law office, with a long-range
                  goal of training for advancement to a position as legal secretary.

EDUCATION

1995 - present   St. Aloysius High School
                  721 West Side Street
                  Jersey City, NJ 07306
                  Expected graduation date: 1999

                  Courses of Study: business law, typing, computer applications, marketing,
                  accounting, Japanese.

                  Current G.P.A.: 3.6

Summer 1998   Drake Secretarial College
                  905 Bergen Avenue
                  Jersey City, NJ 07306

                  Studied shorthand, dictation, and standard business systems.

**WORK
EXPERIENCE**

6/98 - 8/98   Receptionist at Law Office of Dupuy, Jakewith, Howard & Taft
                  Worked as summer replacement receptionist. Responsible for
                  operating telephone switchboard for an office of eight attorneys,
                  six legal assistants, five legal secretaries, and three law clerks.
                  Organized computer mail software installation on all office
                  computers. Typed legal documents as needed.

9/96 - 6/98   Student Office Assistant at Aloysius High School
                  Worked in the high school office, answered telephones, greeted
                  visitors, and assisted school secretaries as needed with filing
                  and typing. Responsible for maintaining daily attendance
                  records for distribution to teachers.

SKILLS   Ability to operate the following: check register, computer (Word Perfect
                  and Lotus 1-2-2), 10-key adding machine.

ACTIVITIES   Future Business Leaders of America, Marketing Club, National Honor
                  Society, and one year of tennis.

REFERENCES   Available on request

JORDAN WILEY
Rural Route 31, Box 243
Cicero, New York 13039
(315) 555-2446

JOB OBJECTIVE

Retail sales position with local merchant.

EDUCATION

Cicero-North Syracuse Senior High School
Rural Route 31, Cicero, NY 13039
Expected graduation date: 1999

Related Courses: Accounting I and II, Business Systems, Math (through Algebra II),
Computer Operations.

Student Training Education Program (STEP)
1421 Stark Street, Syracuse, NY 13029

Related Courses: Personal Finance

WORK HISTORY

Chums Cafe, 1/5/96 - 6/25/97
204 NE Second, Syracuse, New York
Supervisor: Ike Jung

Little Caesar Restaurant, 7/12/95 - 1/2/96
1835 NE Division, Syracuse, New York
Supervisor: Sandra Pommerville

ACTIVITIES

Offices Held	Secretary, Future Business Leaders of America, 1997 President, Bike & Hike Club, 1996-1997
Committees	Homecoming, 1997 - 1998; Junior and Senior Prom Committee, 1996 -1997
Memberships	Cub Scouts, 1986 - 1990; Bike & Hike Club, 1995 - 1998; Youth Convention, 1995 - 1997; Syracuse Swiss Sportsman Club, 1984 - 1996
Sports	Football, 1993 -1997; Indoor Track, 1997 - 1998

References available on request

DAVID JAKES
2390 N. Harvey, No.1
Baltimore, Maryland 21225
(503) 555-6870

OBJECTIVE

Obtain an entry-level position in a business where my organizational and leadership skills can help make a positive difference.

EDUCATION

Douglas High School
Expected graduation date: June 1999

RELATED COURSEWORK

Personal Finance, Career Education, Marketing, Computer Keyboarding.
Current G.P.A.: 3.28

EXPERIENCE & SKILLS DEVELOPMENT

*Promote sales of martial arts merchandise and karate lessons.
*Assist with office operations, answer telephones, schedule lesson times,
 assist students and clients.
*Teach Kenpo Karate, Thai Boxing, and Freestyle Sparring to children and adults,
 in both private and group class situations.
*Distribute flyers to individuals on college campuses and in mall parking lots.
*Abilities include sales, telephone communications, computer keyboarding,
 organization, and customer service.

WORK HISTORY

Baltimore Kenpo Karate School, 1997 - present

REFERENCES

Available on request

Kim Gravenstein
111 N.E. 92nd
Lexington, Kentucky 40503
(606) 555-4900

Job Objective	Part-time secretarial support services.

Education

1994 - 1998	Bryan Station Senior High School

Courses of study:
keyboarding I and II
office systems
two years of business

Work History

1996 - present	*Child Care Provider* Rock Creek Lanes, Lexington

Duties: provide quality childcare in playroom and maintain records and billing for childcare.

1994 - 1996	*Child Care Provider* Private Individuals

Duties: provided full-time summer care for two children in a private home and frequent intermittent evening and weekend care.

Office Skills	Ability to operate the following: computer word processing (75 w.p.m., IBM Word Perfect), ten-key adding machine.
References	Available on request

Jackson Garvey
1134 N.E. 14th
El Dorado, Kansas 67402
(316) 555-3086

Career Goal

My short-term objective is to obtain a position as a warehouseman. For the long-term, my goal is to complete college training in engineering and manufacturing.

Education

El Dorado High School, McCullom Road, El Dorado

> *Courses studied:* metal shop, computer applications, three years of woodworking, and three-dimensional design.

Work Experience

Warehouse Worker for Gates Tire Company, El Dorado, Kansas, *June to August 1998*
> Assisted with receiving shipments, stocking, and sending shipments. Drove forklift and operated loading dock.

Landscape Maintenance for private individuals. *June to August 1997*
> Planted and removed plants and provided lawn maintenance for a variety of personal clients.

Field Worker for Townsend Farms, Inc., *June to August 1996*
> Planting and harvesting for several crops for small family farm operation.

Skills

Able to operate the following: lathe, table saw, drill press, sander, bench grinder, arc welder, Hyster 2450 forklift.

Activities

Junior varsity and varsity baseball and soccer. Member of Greater El Dorado Soccer Club.

References

Available on request.

Shelley Tabor

78 N.E. Towbridge
Bridgewater, Massachusetts 02324
(508) 555-8281

Objective

Assistant position with preschool or child care facility.

Education

Bridgewater-Raynham Regional High School, Mt. Prospect Street.
Expected graduation date 1999.

Specialized Courses: Early Childhood Development, Childhood Education/Preschool, Human Development, Preschool Practicum (hands-on experience in the day care/ preschool), Health and First Aid.

Relevant Work Experience

1993-present
Child-care provider for various private individuals. For two summers, provided full-time care for three children, ages 18 months to 6 years.

1997-present
Supervisor and Assistant, Girl Scout Troop #475. Help to organize and plan activities. Coached troop softball team summer of 1998.

1997-1998
Group Leader, 4-H, Sheep Division. Worked with group of six 5th and 6th grade students to raise Hampshire sheep. Sponsored sheep at state fair in Springfield.

References

Available on request.

Jennifer Hartshore

17327 N.E. Waterton ~ Boston, Massachusetts 02215 ~ 617-555-2239

Job Desired

Part-time secretarial position.

Education

September 1998 - present
Wheelock College, 200 Riverway, Boston

Course of study: Business Management, Accounting, Finance.

1993 - 1998
Cathedral High School, 74 Union Park Street, Boston

Courses taken: Typing II, Office Systems and Procedures, Marketing I, Computer Applications, Spanish IV, Accounting II, and Business Law.

August - October 1995
Academy One Modeling Course

Work Experience

September 1996 - present
Typist at Opti-Craft Laboratory, Inc., Boston

June - August 1995 and 1996
Secretarial Assistant at Barker Enterprises, Inc.

June - August 1994
Attendant at Bruce & Bill's Arco Station

Skills

Ability to operate the following: cash register, ten-key adding machine, IBM computer (Works word processing software, 70 w.p.m.), and dictaphone.

Activities

Future Business Leaders of America, National Honor Society, one year of team volleyball

References

Available on request.

JANINE HARTLEY
168 N.E. Clarkston
Battle Creek, Michigan 49017
Telephone: 616-555-3420
E-Mail: JHart@aol.com

JOB SOUGHT   Position in retail sales for hardware or electronic products.

EDUCATION

1994 - 1998
Battle Creek Central High School, Battle Creek, Michigan

Specialized coursework:
Marketing I
Spanish IV
Accounting II
Electronics
Woodworking Shop

WORK EXPERIENCE

11/96 - present
Battle Creek Auto Parts
Duties: serving customers, maintaining warehouse supply, stocking
and shelving parts, receiving shipments. (Left when store closed).

2/95 - 10/96
Wendy's Store #1023
Duties: fast food preparation, order processing, clean-up and operation
of kitchen machinery.

ACTIVITIES

Outdoor school counselor, one year of basketball.

REFERENCES

Available on request.

JUAN AGUILAR

158 Halladay S.W.
Benton Harbor, Michigan 49028   Telephone: 616-555-7379

Job Desired

Printer's apprentice in newspaper printing department

Education

1995 - present
Benton Harbor High School; Expected graduation date: June 1999.

Pertinent courses: graphic arts, journalism, photography, computer science

Skills & Experience

Ability to operate the following: Graphic printing press, screen printer, camera, copy machine, Compugraphic 2824 typesetter, Macintosh computer (Quark Xpress, PageMaker, Adobe Photoshop, Aldus Freehand).

Work Experience

Production chief for Harbor High Herald. 1997 - present.

Duties include set-up and layout of boards for printing preparation. Successfully completed transfer from traditional typesetting and layout to electronic pre-press with ability to scan photographs into system, then crop and size electronically to fit layout of text and other graphics.

Printing assistant for Michigan Printing. Summer 1998.

Assisted with preparing camera-ready mechanicals for film, making photo negatives for printing plates, positioning plates on press, checking press runs, operating cutter and folder, Worked with stripping department on cutting masks and windows in film.

House painting for private residence, interior and exterior. Summers of 1996 and 1997.

References

Available on request.

Michelle M. Hibbard
3320 Delaware Avenue
Erie, New York 14222
(716) 555-2193

Education

1996 - present   Marshfield Girls Academy, 24 Shoshone Street, Erie, New York

1987 - present   Private voice lessons; Roseanne Valdivieso and Pauline Jenson, Erie

1986 - 1992   Ballet lessons, Judy Andresch School of Dance, Erie

Experience

1997 - present: der Rheinlander Restaurant, Academy Boulevard, Erie
Singing Hostess. Greet and seat customers, and provide musical entertainment.

1997 - present: Balloons, Etc., West McKinley Parkway, Erie
Delivery Person. Drive company van to deliver balloon bouquets, flowers, and singing telegrams.

1994 - present: Providing childcare in private homes, Erie
Care for children ages 2 to 7, provide meals and first aid.

1991 - present: Singing in private weddings and at private parties, Erie.

Achievements

First soloist for the Eire County Youth Choir, 1996 and 1997
Marshfield Girls' Choir, 1996 - present
Marshfield Dance Team, Captain, 1998
Youth of the Month, Erie Elks Lodge No. 125, January 1997
Junior Class President, 1997-1998
National Honor Society Scholar of the Year, 1998
State Letter in girls' volleyball
Speak conversational German

References

Available upon request.

Brandon Smith

317 W. Trinity, Apt. 6
Durham, North Carolina   Telephone: (704) 555-2930

Education

Hillside High School, 1900 Concord Street, Durham
Expected graduation date: 1999

Durham Technical Community College, Special Summer Session
Attended Summer 1998, pre-engineering

Relevant Training

Three years of Math (through Trigonometry), Practical Physics, Chemistry, Woods II, Metals II, and Building Construction.

Experience and Skills

Assisted with framing and roofing two new houses. Completed roof repair project on cedar-shake roof. Removed and replaced siding on one wall of shingle-sided house.

Provided landscape maintenance for private homes, including lawn mowing, weeding, trimming, hedging, and some planting.

Through school coursework I have developed the ability to operate a lathe, table saw, drill press, and other metal and woodworking machinery, as well as typewriter, IBM computer (word processing and DISCOVER software), and HP 95X scientific calculator.

Work Record

John Jalletty Construction, 421 Driver Street, Durham; June-August 1997

Hillside High School, Wood Shop Assistant, Durham; September 1997-June 1998

References

Available on request.

GARY LUPAS
809 N. Washington Street
Bismarck, North Dakota 58501
Telephone: 555-3994

OBJECTIVE

Position in agribusiness utilizing my supervisory and organizational skills.

EDUCATION

Central Senior High School, 1000 East Century Avenue, Bismarck
    Diploma awarded 1998

        Courses completed: business series courses in agriculture, law, and marketing;
        special project course in which I devised and prepared a marketing and development
        plan for a new agricultural support services business.

RELEVANT EXPERIENCE

Hay Bailer/Field Boss, Klair & Klock Larson Farm. Summers 1995-1997
    Worked each summer in berry fields, earning at the top 10 percent of all field hands
    (paid by ton bailed). In 1997, I was hired as a field boss and was responsible for
    supervising workers, paying fees, and checking for quality.

Swim Instructor/Life Guard, Bismarck Community Pool. *9/96-6/97*
    Supervised swim activities at indoor pool facility. Taught swimming lessons to 4th,
    5th, and 6th grade children. Hold current life-saving certificate.

SKILLS & ACTIVITIES

        Experienced with wide range of farm implements and machinery.
        Valid driver's license.
        Swim team member (first place in state competition).

REFERENCES

        Available on request.

ERIN R. DURANT
223 Brittain Road
Redmond, Washington 98052
(206) 555-3380

EDUCATION

Redmond Senior High School: Expected graduation date: 1999

Specialized Courses: Home building construction, PGE Good Sense Home, Wood Shop, Auto Technology. (4.0 G.P.A. in these areas).

SKILLS

As a result of both regular and freelance employment, I have gained specific job-related skills in the following areas: logging, wood cutting, pipe laying, heavy equipment operation, carpentry, general house repair and maintenance, yard work, house painting, automotive repair.

WORK EXPERIENCE

Laborer for Jenson Building Management, September 1998
Stripped and replumbed a bathroom, cleaned gutters, installed insulation, removed shrubbery.

Laborer for Scott Farris (Private Contractor), summers of 1997 and 1998
Completed deck repairs, washed and painted buildings, trimmed trees, shored up a retaining wall. Also involved with roof repair, window cleaning, car repair, and moving and transportation.

Laborer for Wolcott Excavating, summers of 1995 and 1996
Worked on ditch digging, ran errands in company truck to obtain pipe and blueprints, made deliveries of pipe and fixtures, read blueprints, installed insulation, took inventory, filled orders, organized stock. Operated chain saw, jumping jack, 580K backhoe, Halton cat loader, Halton cat D4, Case 24-ton roller, and drove dump truck.

I have also worked on several other short-term contractor jobs doing carpentry and general labor.

ACTIVITIES

Four years wrestling letterman, two years football, track official for the track teams, student government, and building construction and wood shop.

References are available upon request.

STEPHANIE TIRRELL
889 Copley Road
Akron, Ohio 44308
Telephone: (216) 555-1941

OBJECTIVE

Because of my love for children and my interest in their development, I am seeking a position as a caregiver in a quality preschool or day care environment.

EDUCATION

Central Hower High School, 123 N. Forge Street, Akron, Ohio 44303
    Expected graduation date: 1999
    Specialized courses: Child Development, Early Childhood Education

Mt. Union College, 1972 Clark Avenue, Akron, Ohio 44601
    Summer of 1998 open enrollment program.
    Courses: Child Development, Beginning Psychology

RELATED EXPERIENCE

Childcare: I have been providing competent childcare since 1993. I provide care consistently for four children in two different families.

Counseling: In October 1996 and April 1997, I worked as a counselor at the Trout Creek Outdoor School, supervising sixth grade students and teaching basic plant identification and plant ecology. Also presented lessons on plants at several grade schools.

Volunteer: Since June 1996 I have offered tours a the Akron Park Zoo, educating children about zoo animals, natural habitat, and endangered species. During October 1997 I participated in the "Zoo Boo" Train. I dressed in costume and entertained train riders along the route.

REFERENCES

Available on request.

Aisha Mgazi
289 Windvale Drive
Pittsburgh, Pennsylvania 15236
Telephone: (412) 555-9027

Job Desired

Sales clerk or customer service representative for major department store.

Education

Baldwin High School, 4653 Clairton Boulevard, Pittsburgh
Graduation date: June 1999

Work Experience

Courtesy Clerk, A&G Food Centers, 181st & Parkfield, April 1996-present
My primary responsibility is to assist customers in locating items and taking purchases to their cars. I also bag groceries, count bottles, stock shelves, and provide additional assistance as needed.

Assistant, Monograms Plus, City Center Mall, Summer 1996 & November 1996 - January 1997
Responsible for monogramming shirts, sweatshirts, shorts, and jackets; providing customer service; and stocking shelves.

Sales Representative, Accents, City Center Mall, November 1994 to January 1995.
Served customers, coordinated sales, operated the cash register, and assisted with maintaining stock.

Skills

Accurately operate a cash register and handle cash and credit card financial transfers. Experienced with IBM-compatible computer word processing software and can type 70 words per minute.

Activities

Served as a counselor at Outdoor School, am a member of International Club and Multicultural Students Organization, have played three years of team volleyball, and work at school track meets.

References

Available upon request.

BRIAN SCHLOSSER

243 Pleasant Avenue   Providence, Rhode Island 02903 401/555-2335

Objective

To obtain part-time employment as a stage hand for theatrical productions in a small theatrical company.

Education

Hope High School. Will graduate in June 1999. Current GPA: 3.3

Shea High School, Pawtucket, Rhode Island. Attended 1996-1997.

Relevant Experience

*Worked as stage manager for three school productions
*Operated lights and sound for musical production of "Oklahoma"
*Assisted with set design and building for three plays
*Experienced with all aspects of theatrical production
*Worked as stage hand for a production at Brown University
*Played the lead in "Brigadoon"
*Sang in the chorus in "Godspell"

Work History

Cashier and line cook for Taco Time, Providence. 4/95 - present.

Paper distributor for the Pawtucket Evening News. 3/95 - 3/97

Activities

Member of Thespian Society. Participated in various aspects of student theatrical productions at Hope High School.

Madrigal Singers and Concert Choir, Shea High School.

References

Available on request.

LEVARR JOHNSON
2230 Cunningham Lane
Clarksville, TN 37042
(615) 555-8117

JOB SOUGHT

Entry-level technician

EDUCATION

Northwest High School, Lafayette Road, Clarksville
Diploma awarded June 1998. Grade point average: 3.87
Major: Technology and Electronics

Civil Air Patrol (U.S. Air Force Auxiliary), 1995 to present

SKILLS

Trained in electronics repair at Civil Air Patrol (oscilloscopes, radios, radar)

Completed two years in technology and electronics courses at Northwest High

Repaired disassembled television set to working order

Experienced in operating compression tools for construction

WORK HISTORY

Construction Worker for Johnson Construction, April 1994 to present.

> *Major duties:* Framed and roofed homes, hauled lumber to job site in company truck, checked lumber delivery against purchase order.

Pizza Chef at Little Caesar's, Clarksville, Tennessee, 1992 to 1994

REFERENCES

Available on request.

Brian McGavin
990 Woody Road
Dallas, TX 75253
(214) 555-2369

OBJECTIVE

A career in business management. Immediate goal is an entry-level position with a growing business.

EDUCATION

Lake Highlands Senior High School. Graduation: May 1999
Specialized Courses:
- Business I & II
- Computer Science (two years)
- Spanish I & II
- Current G.P.A.: 3.0

EXPERIENCE

Assistant Manager, Taco Bell Restaurant, May 1998 to present
Started as line cook, June 1996; promoted to cashier, November 1996; promoted to manager with supervisory responsibility May 1998.

Assistant Manager, Student Store, Lake Highlands Senior High, September 1996 to June 1997
Responsible for scheduling workers for student store operation. Checked accuracy of cash reports and tracked any discrepancies. Assisted manager with ordering stock and receiving shipments.

Student Assistant, Counseling Office, Lake Highlands Senior High, September 1995 to June 1996
Worked for four counselors, answered telephones, scheduled appointments, typed letters. Student assistants were selected on basis of ability, skills, and trustworthiness.

ACTIVITIES

- Future Business Leaders of America
- DECA (Diversified Education Clubs of America, a marketing club)
- Attended Texas Business Week at American Institute of Commerce, Dallas, Texas
- Currently Vice President of DECA, which operates the student store at Lake Highland Senior High School.

REFERENCES

Available on Request

Tammy Pryde
2339 S.E. Kibling Avenue
Tyler, Texas 75710
(214) 555-0422

Job Sought

Summer internship in graphic design that will utilize my computer drawing and layout skills and provide opportunities for further training.

Education

Lee High School. Anticipated graduate date: May 1999
- art and graphics (three years)
- computer applications
- drafting/mechanical drawing
- current GPA: 3.29

Work Experience

Graphic Artist, student publications (newspapers, yearbook)
- Designed logos and mastheads.
- Established design formats for entire newspaper.
- Worked with design and production team to design yearbook.
- Designed yearbook cover.
- Set up computer templates on Macintosh using Publish-It Easy.
- Worked with editors on layout of each issue of the newspaper.
- Designed advertisements for student clubs for both publications.
- Created new computer clip art and altered existing art, using Claris MacPaint and MacDraw programs.

References are available on request.

Sherria Gonzalez

235 Gramercy Avenue   Ogden, Utah 84404   801-555-1409

Objective

Obtain a summer internship with a local business so that I may utilize my clerical skills and learn more about personnel issues. My long-term goal is a career in personnel management.

Education

Lamond High School, Ogden   Class of 2000

Courses pertinent to job objective: business and economics, computer applications, typing, career education. GPA: 3.28.
Currently serving as a counseling office assistant, where I answer telephones, type file, and schedule appointments.

Work Experience

Wimpy's Burgers, 560 N.W. Phoenix Drive, Ogden   1997 to present
Responsibilities: serve customers, prepare food, operate cash register, handle money, close store.

Jazzercise, 2466 E. Burns, Ogden   1997 to present
Responsibilities: provide quality care for children of parents participating in Jazzercise exercise programs.

Skills

I am experienced with Macintosh and IBM computers, and I have good typing (70 wpm), filing, and telephone communications skills. I am also a quick learner and strive to be accurate in everything I do. Fluent Spanish speaker.

References

Available on request.

Kendra Wallen

1137 N.E. 189th, Provo, UT 84606   (801) 555-2740

OBJECTIVE

Student teaching for summer at art camp programs.

EDUCATION

Timpview High School, Class of 1999
Courses include: childhood education, Art (two years), advanced studio painting,
and computer applications in art.

EXPERIENCE

Since June of 1994, I have worked as a child care provider to children of various ages,
responsible for preparing food, feeding, diapering, and general care. Each summer I
worked full-time and offered innovative children's art projects that were designed for
specific ages and abilities.

In June of 1996 and 1997 I taught art during vacation Bible school program for elementary
school children on the Navajo Reservation.

SPECIAL SKILLS

Ability to operate a variety of computer software and hardware programs, specifically
programs providing graphic arts and page layout capabilities. Hold valid CPR card.

References and portfolio of children's projects are available on request.

15 Church Street
Rutland, Virginia 05701
(802) 555-1939

Aki Mioshi

Job Sought

Department store security staff position, working evenings or weekends.

Education

Rutland High School, 67 Library Avenue, Rutland
Class of 1999
Current GPA: 3.7

State Police Explorer Program
Attended: Summer 1995

Accomplishments

- Started RADD, Rutlanders Against Drugs and Drinking
- Elected Vice-President of Junior Class, Rutland High School
- Lettered in track and field, volleyball, and softball
- Listed on Honor Roll every semester since Freshman year
- Fluent in spoken Japanese

Work History

Waitress: The Pines Restaurant, Rutland   10/97 - present
Duties: greet and serve customers, communicate orders to kitchen staff, direct preparation of salads and deserts. Responsible for quality of service provided to customers. Earned bonus for excellence and courtesy, December 1997.

References are available on request.

V i n   Q u a m   P h o n g

1321 Longview Drive, Woodbridge, Virginia 22192   703-555-4958

O b j e c t i v e

Entry-level graphic arts or production position

E x p e r i e n c e

Garfield News
Production Chief, 1997-1998
Graphic Artist, 1996-1997

Created layout for student newspaper. Designed advertisements. Prepared paste-up boards for printing. Sized and cropped photographs for reproduction. Specified type sizes and styles for typesetters. Selected and designed art images to enhance visual design of newspaper. Worked with editorial staff to determine placement of news articles and photographs.

Freelance Artist
1996-present

Designed and prepared mechanicals for logo for my father's restaurant supply business. Drew portraits at State Fair. Worked for several student groups to design banners, signs, and logos for school-related activities.

E d u c a t i o n

Garfield High School. Anticipated date of graduation: 1999.

My elective coursework has focused on art and design, often involving extracurricular projects because I had completed the class assignments and sought additional opportunities to challenge my skills. Art and Design GPA: 4.0.

R e f e r e n c e s

Available on request

JASON RAINTREE
2268-A 187th Street
Seattle, Washington 98055
(206) 555-9225

OBJECTIVE   Summer internship with social service agency

EDUCATION

Tyee High School, 4224 S. 188th Street, Seattle
Graduation Class of 1998
Cumulative Grade Point Average: 3.47

Course work designed to provide broad background with some specific training in areas useful to social services, including:

>   *child development
>   *sociology
>   *psychology
>   *writing for business
>   *U.S. government
>   *Spanish (three years)

EXPERIENCE & ACHIEVEMENTS

Volunteer assistant at Boys and Girls Club of South Seattle. Coached and refereed elementary school children on sports teams, including basketball, soccer, and softball. Helped counselors with "Just Say No" educational programs.

Coordinated, with three other students, an anti-drug club that sponsored alcohol and drug-free events and activities as well as an annual drug awareness assembly. Our goal was to increase the status of being drug-free. In the first year, we had 50 percent participation throughout the school.

Selected by South Seattle Rotary Club International to present an essay celebrating Seattle's Native American heritage and proposing some remedies for the problems facing Native Americans in today's society.

REFERENCES are available on request.

Robert Goldstein
2250 Collins Avenue
Huntington, West Virginia 25702
Telephone: 304-555-9941

Job Sought	Training position with Huntington Fire District.
Education	<u>Cabel County Vocational-Technical Senior High</u> Diploma. Class of 1998. Major: Health and Physical Education. Courses: health and human fitness, human anatomy, safety and first aid, human development.
Experience	<u>Referee</u>, West Hills Soccer Club, 1994 - present. Work during summers and on weekends to referee soccer games and tournaments for elementary and junior high school level soccer teams. <u>Referee and Ticket Sales</u>, CCVTSHS, 1994 - 1996. Served as practice referee during basketball team practice sessions. Sold tickets at entrance for some basketball games.
Activities & Awards	President's Council on Physical Fitness, first award Varsity football, letter award Varsity track and field, letter award
References	Available on request.

Anjala Hindagolla
2325 Rapids Drive
Racine, Wisconsin 53406
(414) 555-8733

Objective	Cook or chef's assistant in Middle Eastern restaurant.
Experience	Ramdalla, Milwaukee Wisconsin, 1994-1997

*Worked in former family restaurant as chef's assistant.
*Operated kitchen machinery
*Prepared foods from recipes.
*Maintained oven and grill cleanliness.
*Prepared serving plates for beautiful visual presentation.
*Gained experience in ass aspects of restaurant food preparation.

Education   Case High School, Racine, Wisconsin, Class of 1993

Specialized courses:

*Home Economics I and II
*Food Science and Nutrition
*Business Operations
*Food Preparation and Safety (special workshop at state health division)

References   Available on request

Darryl J. Richmond
356 N. Alameda
Santa Rosa, California 95406
(707) 555-3964

Objective   Summer carpenter crew position with home construction company.

Experience   Tiara Construction Company
5316 S.E. Francis, Sebastapol, California 95472
Summer 1996 and 1997
Supervisor: George Linde, (707) 555-5015

Worked with carpentry crew; famed and roofed houses; sheetrocked interiors; installed insulation in walls and rafters.

Growers Outlet, Stocker
15165 S.E. Laguna Blvd., Santa Rosa, California 95403
September 1996 to present
Supervisor: Janet Brendler, (707) 555-2000

Work with grocery supervisor to stock shelves, receive and direct shipments of produce, maintain quality presentation in produce department.

Education   Santa Rosa High School
2156 Cerritos, Santa Rosa, California 95401
Expected graduation date: 1999

Pertinent courses: wood and metal shop, building construction, mechanical drawing, architecture.

Santa Rosa Middle School
1800 Terra Blvd., Santa Rosa, California 95401

Pertinent courses: wood shop.

References   Available on request.

Janice Anne Richland
10205 Catlin Avenue
Brookline, Massachusetts 02146
(617) 555-0116

Objective

Retail sales position with music store

Skills

Good knowledge of both contemporary an classical music. Work well with people. Able to operate cash registers and most office equipment.

Work Experience

Cashier Wendy's Hamburger Restaurant, Thayer Road, Brookline
    Supervisor: Raejean Matthews (617) 555-9444
    June 1997 to present

Duties Greet customers, take orders, communicate orders to line cooks, operate cash register, handle cash, close and balance register receipts at shift's end.

Clerical
Assistant Brookline High School, Main Office
    Supervisor: Annette Jameson (617) 555-7800
    Summer 1996

Duties Answered telephones, routed calls through six-line switchboard, typed letters, filed, greeted visitors, assisted teachers and students as needed.

Education

Brookline High School, Brookline, Massachusetts
    Expected graduation date: June 1999
    Pertinent Courses: Wind ensemble, orchestra, jazz band, choir, music theory, business.

Standish Middle School, Boston, Massachusetts
    September 1994 - June 1996
    Pertinent Courses: Concert band, jazz band.

Achievements

First place league solo 1998; four Outstanding Solo Jazz awards 1997-1998; MAME Youth Series O.S.O. 1997; All-State Band 1997; Honor Roll student.

References Available

Masoud Ysmirir
211 South Grevillea Avenue, Apt. 26B
Inglewood California 90301
(213) 555-9562

Objective	Career in electronics design and manufacturing.
Education	Morningside High School, Class of 1998 Cumulative Grade Point Average: 3.9 Pertinent Courses: *Electronics *Computer Applications *Algebra I and II *Trigonometry *Precalculus
Experience	Assistant to Electronics Teacher, Morningside High School. Dates: 1996-1998 Completed all available course work in electronics. Functioned as lab instructor during beginning electronics courses.
Achievements	Developed radar device for activating electronic control panel. Coordinated project for lighting student theater. Built and operated control board for sound and light productions. Built and customized computer hard disk drive for personal computer. Experienced in repair of stereos, video cassette recorders, and CD players.
References	Available on request.

LYNN SIMMONS
2620 Harrison Avenue
Cheyenne, Wyoming 82001
Telephone: 307-555-2883

JOB SOUGHT:	Summer firefighting crew.
EDUCATION:	Central Senior High School 5500 Education Drive, Cheyenne, Wyoming 82001 Graduation date: June 1999
TRAINING:	Hold vaild CPR/Lifesaving Certificate Trained in firefighting and prevention by Cheyenne County Fire Department
EXPERIENCE:	U.S. Forest Service, Summer 1998 Spent two weeks with fire crew in Yellowstone National Park on fire damage control. Dug fire trenches, cleared brush, and opened clogged stream beds. U.S. Forest Service, Summer 1997 Worked as camp cook's assistant on fire crew on site in Yellowstone National Park. Maintained food provisions for firefighters, assisted with first aid treatment of minor burns, served meals, worked at camp canteen.
REFERENCES:	Available at your request.

JOHN UMIAK
P.O. Box 1648
Palmer, Alaska 99645
Message phone: 907-555-8406

Objective   Career in fisheries and wildlife.

Education   Sustina Valley Junior-Senior High School
                             Graduation date: May 1998. G.P.A. 3.6.

                             Courses were primarily in biological sciences, with an emphasis in
                             special projects on salmonid fishes.

                             Matanuska-Sustina College

                             Enrolled in 1998 summer program, took courses in general biology and
                             marine biology.

Experience   Matanuska Fisheries, June 1998-present

                             Work on fishing boat crew, fishing for salmon, halibut, crab. Maintain
                             fishing equipment, check fishing nets daily for damage and repair them
                             as needed.

                             Independent project, 1997-1998

                             Coordinated research project on salmon runs in local stream. Working
                             with my high school biology teacher, I designed research procedures,
                             collected data, and discovered a 20% decrease in salmon populations
                             between 1991 and 1992 spring Chinook runs.

References   Available on request.

AMANDA MARTIN
1076 North 27th
Phoenix, Arizona 85028
(602) 555- 3874

GOAL: A career in the computer industry.

EDUCATION: Shadow Mountain High School, 1994-1998
                    Cumulative G.P.A.: 3.75

                    Relevant Courses:
                    Computer Science
                    Computer Applications
                    Computer Programming (BASIC, PASCAL)
                    Alegebra
                    Geometry
                    Trigonometry
                    Precalculus

ACHIEVEMENTS: Worked on five-member team to develop new computer
                    software for grading multiple-choice tests, recording grades,
                    and providing bell curves and other averages that could be used
                    for assigning letter grades.

                    Customized programming software for use by students with
                    visual impairments.

                    Won annual district prize for best computer programming
                    solution.

REFERENCES: Available upon request.

Paul Garcia
3826 Sweetwater Avenue
Scottsdale, Arizona 85254
(602) 555-2834

Objective: Summer internship with law office.

Education: Chaparral High School, class of 1998
                  Academic standing: 20th in class of 420
                  Cumulative grade point average: 4.0

                  Courses taken:
                  Business Law
                  Business Practices
                  Computer Applications (word processing, spreadsheets,
                     databases)
                  Journalism
                  Career Options: Law

Achievements: BPOE Elks Scholarship
                  Zimmerman Scholarship
                  Student of the Month, Scottsdale Elks Club
                  President, National Honor Society
                  Student Senator, sophomore and junior years
                  Chaparral High Scholarship & Leadership Award
                  Dean's Honor Roll
                  Member: Chaparral Thespians, Scottsdate First Methodist
                          Youth Choir, Chaps (high school jazz ensemble)

References: Available on request.

Jerome Washington
3705 H Street
Little Rock, Arkansas
501-555-3785

Objective

A career in computer programming and development

Education

McClellan High School. Graduation Date: May 1998
Cumulative Grade Point Average: 3.98

Relevant Courses

Computer Programming
(BASIC, PASCAL, DOS)
Computer Applications
(Microsoft Word, Lotus 1-2-3, dBase, Symphony, Microsoft Works)
Electronics (including microchip technology)
Four years of math

Honors

McClellan Senior Scholarship
Little Rock Masonic Scholarship
Most Innovative Computer Solution Award, cBasic Magazine
Elected Treasurer, Computer J's Club

Work History

Waiter, Genrette's Ice Cream Parlor, 1996-1998
Station Attendant, Scott's Chevron, 1995-1996

REFERENCES AVAILABLE

SHAWANA HARRIS
110 Royal Scots Way, Apt. 245
Bakersfield, California 93306
Telephone: (805) 555-3746
Messages: (805) 555-8892

OBJECTIVE   Customer service job with computer company.

EDUCATION   Foothill High School, 501 Park Drive, Bakersfield
Expected graduation date: June 1999
Current G.P.A.: 3.2

Special courses: Computer Applications (Microsoft Works, WordPerfect, Corel Draw), Business Applications, Accounting.

Special activities: Served as clerical assistant for English teachers. Worked as a clerk in the student store. Planned and carried out activities as part of the Homecoming and Senior Prom committees. Played varsity basketball (top scorer last season). Made the honor roll 4 out of 6 semesters.

EXPERIENCE   *Student Assistant,* FHS Computer Lab, 1997-1998.
Worked with computer teacher. Installed and initialized software on lab computers. Maintained student use records for lab. Assisted students with questions about computer software. Supervised checkout of lab materials.

Waitress, Michael's Landing Restaurant, 1996-1998.

REFERENCES   Available on request.

SHARONE DAVIS
22200 Division Street, Apt. 315
Los Angeles, California 93535
(805) 555-3736

OBJECTIVE   Entry-level position with production department of
newspaper or printing firm.

EDUCATION   Antelope Valley High School, class of 1998
Cumulative grade point average: 3.48

Pertinent courses: Photography, Darkroom Techniques,
Graphic Design, Introduction to Art, Mechanical Drawing.

EXPERIENCE   Darkroom Technician, Antelope High School,
Viewpoint (student newspaper), 1997-1998
Duties: developed, proofed, and printed black-and-white
film; prepared PMTs of line art in specified enlargements
and reductions; made halftoned prints for direct paste-up;
made negatives to size for stripping into plate-ready film.

Layout Artist, Antelope High School
Viewpoint, 1996-1997
Duties: Responsible for computerized layout of paper
using Macintosh computer and Quark XPress layout
software.

REFERENCES   are available on request.

Michael Han
435 S. Monaco Parkway
Denver, Colorado 80204
(303) 555-4481

Education

West High School, 951 Elati Street, Denver, 1994-1998. Diploma. G.P.A.: 3.86.

Aachen Gymnasium, Bonn, West Germany, 1996-1997 (Exchange Student).

Skills & Achievements

*Trained in basic bookkeeping, invoicing, inventory, and payroll procedures.
*Speak fluent Chinese and German; working knowledge of French.
*Experienced with various computer software and hardware, including MS DOS, Macintosh,
  and CP/M operating platforms; WordPerfect, Microsoft Word, and MacWrite word
  processing; Lotus 1-2-3 and Works spreadsheet; and dBase and Filemaker Pro
  Database software, among others.
*Experienced with providing customer service in small retail sales outlet for computer
  equipment.
*Excellent writing and communications skills.
*Effective leadership skills; served as president of senior class, vice-president of junior
  class, student senator during first and second years.
*Selected by American Field Service (AFS) as exchange student to Aachen, West Germany.

Employment History

Summer Sales Intern, Computer Express, Denver, Winter 1997-1998.
  Duties: Provided information and assistance to clients in small computer hardware
  and software dealership that handled both IBM and compatibles and Macintosh
  computers. Self-trained in a wide range of software in order to better match
  appropriate software and hardware systems to clients' needs.

REFERENCES AVAILABLE

Mark Bettorini
2100 West Oxford Avenue
Englewood, Colorado 80110
(303) 555-3422

Objective   Career in forestry/wood products industry that will utilize my science background, timber experience, and leadership skills.

Experience   Fire Watch/Tree Planter, U.S. Forest Service, Denver. Summer 1998.

Crew Leader, Colorado Highway Department, Grounds Crew.
Summer 1997.

Education   Sheridan High School, Englewood
Class of 1999
Major: Science

Leadership   Student Body Vice-President, Sheridan High School, 1997-1998.
President, Sheridan Hikers Club, 1996-1997.
President, American Junior Red Cross, 1998.
Vice-President, Science Club, 1996-1998
Captain, Sheridan High School Archery Team, 1997-1998.
Founding Member, Sheridan High Key Club (volunteer service agency), 1996.

Honors   Junior Science Student of the Year, 1998.
Rotary Club International Exchange Student to New Zealand, spring 1997.
Key Club Volunteer of the Month, December 1997.

References are available on request.

JUDY REIMER
128 Orange Street
New Haven, CT 06510
(203) 555-3754

OBJECTIVE

To secure a position as a paralegal where my education and writing and research skills can be utilized to enhance the effectiveness of a small- to medium-sized law firm.

EDUCATION

Hillhouse High School, 480 Sherman Parkway, New Haven; diploma awarded May 1998.

Concentration: Business, Accounting I and II, Computer Applications (word processing, spreadsheet, database, and communications software for MS DOS operating platforms), Business Operations (clerical systems). Cumulative G.P.A.: 3.75.

EXPERIENCE

Office Assistant. Switter, Harvey, Jenkins & Hewitt, Attorneys at Law, 1996-present.

Duties: Assisted attorneys and legal secretaries. Typed and proofed legal forms. Answered telephone calls on ten-line switchboard. Organized office law library and reshelved books.

Student Assistant. Hillhouse High School, Attendance Office, 1995-1996.

Duties: Assisted staff secretaries with typing filing, answering telephones, and duplication. Distributed mail to teachers and administrators. Distributed work orders to teachers. Operated stencil machine, photocopier, fax, and six-line switchboard.

ACTIVITIES & ACHIEVEMENTS

Secretary, National Honor Society, 1997-1998
Senior Editor, Sheridan High School Annual, 1997-1998
Team Captain, Sheridan Girls Softball Team, 1997-1998
Copy Editor, Shericdan High School Annual, 1996-1997
Member, Future Business Leaders of America, 1994-1996
Member, Thespians (participated in three theatrical productions), 1994-1997

REFERENCES

Available on request

STUART J. ECK
126 S. Granby
Hartford, Connecticut 06112
203-555-6623

EDUCATION: Buckley High School, 300 Wethersfield Avenue, Hartford Class of 1999

Hold 4.0 grade point average in all math, business, writing, and English courses.

Recipient of Who's Who Among American High School Students.

LEADERSHIP: Presided over Business Club. Planned programs, managed budget, set meeting agendas, and organized meetings and club activities, 1997-1998.

Elected Secretary of the Student Senate. Responsible for maintaining Robert's Rules of Order, 1997-1998.

Managed budget, personnel time sheets, and all-school database or student publication. Used Microsoft Works software on Macintosh computers, 1997-1998.

Received full scholarship to attend Student Government Conference at State Capitol, summer 1996.

Supervised volunteer labor while working at Hartford's Capitol grounds, spring 1996.

EXPERIENCE: *Business Manager*, The Hart (student annual), 1997-1998.

Groundskeeper, Buckley High School, 1995-1998.

Corpsmember, U.S. Federal Government, Youth Conservation Corps, 1995-1997.

REFERENCES AVAILABLE UPON REQUEST

Craig Kohanek
1851 S. Edwards Road, No. 59
Wilmington, Delaware 19809
302-555-7229; Message: 302-555-1762

OBJECTIVE

To obtain a position in sales in an organization oriented toward customer service.

EDUCATION

Mount Pleasant High School, Washington Boulevard, Wilmington. Class of 1999.

Course of study: Business I and II (organizational structures, economics of business, business ethics, business law, personnel management, business regulations), Computer Systems (software applications in word processing, database management, accounting, and communications), Office Management (clerical operations, bookkeeping, basic accounting).

EXPERIENCE

Library Assistant, Mt. Pleasant High School Library, Wilmington. January 1996-present. Organize and record use of magazines in periodicals section. Instruct students on library research techniques and microfilm usage. Answer questions. Maintain copy machine. Reshelve books.

Cashier, Hartford Country Club Golf Shop, Hartford. June-September 1997. Sold rounds of golf, clubs, shoes, and miscellaneous equipment. Monitored driving range. Supervised and participated in cleaning and maintenance of club house.

Retail Sales Clerk, Stan's Shoe Shop, Hartford. June-September 1995 and 1996. Trained in sales and customer service. Greeted customers, took measurements, assisted with style and color selection, ran cash register. Received and accounted for delivered merchandise on corresponding purchase orders and invoices. Designed and set up seasonal displays.

LEADERSHIP EXPERIENCE

Student Tutor, Mt. Pleasant High School, English classes, 1995-1998.
Student Representative, Mt. Pleasant High School Senate, 1996-1998
Competitor, Mt. Pleasant High School Forensics Squad, 1995-1998.
Representative, Mt. Pleasant High School Model United Nations, 1998.

EXTRACURRICULAR ACTIVITIES

Varsity Basketball, Mt. Pleasant High School, 1996-1998
Varsity Cross Country, 1996-1998
Concert Choir, First United Church, 1993-present

REFERENCES AVAILABLE ON REQUEST

Mary Jo Baptiste
2240 N.W. Nebraska Avenue
Washington, D.C. 20016
202-555-7465

OBJECTIVE

To obtain a training position as a preschool guide in a Montessori preschool.

EDUCATIONAL BACKGROUND

Coolidge High School, Washington, D.C.
Graduation Date: June 1998

Relevant Courses: Human Development, Childhood Education, Psychology, Sociology, Social Science, Speech and Communications.

Honors: Who's Who Among American High School Students, Future Teachers of America, Volunteer Student Activist of the Year (all-school nomination), District of Columbia Youth of the Month (President's Council on Youth), Quill and Scroll (journalism honor society).

EXPERIENCE

Parks & Recreation Day Camp Leader, Washington, D.C., Summer 1996 and 1997.
Planned programs for children 4-8 years old. Built rapport and communications with parents. Provided supervision of children on play structures during breaks. Taught teamwork skills through problem solving in groups of six children. Taught crafts, songs, and dances. Led storytelling for children aged 10-14.

Outdoor School Counselor and Instructor, D.C. School District, 1995-1997.
Counseled, supervised, and instructed sixth-grade students from various Washington elementary schools during one-week program each spring. Assumed responsibility for twelve girls. Served as live-in counselor three years, one year as instructor emphasizing environmental education.

Other part-time employment: Waitress, housekeeper, clerical assistant.

SPECIAL SKILLS AND INTERESTS

Reporter on the high school newspaper staff for two years. Published an article in the *City Paper*, Washington, D.C., February 1998. Knowledge of Native American culture, including traditional songs, dances, and crafts.

References are available upon request.

Jeanette Bouchardon
21 Lawrence Street N.W.
Washington, D.C. 20017
(202) 555-2951

Objective To obtain a position in international business where my bilingual skills and experience in sales and customer service will be used to advantage.

Experience Holiday Inn Corporation, Washington, 1997 and 1998 (summers)
Assistant Night Manager
*Assisted with translation for French-speaking guests
*Coordinated night-shift activities
*Managed front-desk operations
*Operated telephone switchboard and reservations desk
*Conducted night audits of front desk register

La Maison Bleu, Washington, 1997-1998 (part-time)
Hostess
*Assisted with translation for French-speaking guests
*Supervised cash register
*Supervised table setting
*Supervised bussing staff

Nordstrom's Department Store, Washington, 1996-1997 (weekends)
Salesperson
*Sold women's sportswear, cosmetics, and jewelry
*Maintained accurate balance sheets, accounting for all sales
*Recipient of August 1997 Sales Award (based on per-work-hour sales)

Education Washington International School, 3100 Macomb Street, N.W., Washington
*Honors student with cumulative grade point average of 5.8 (6.0 scale).
*Anticipated date of graduation: May 1999.

Special Skills *Fluent French speaker (child of French parents; mother member of Corps Diplomatique)
*Excellent interpersonal communications skills
*General knowledge of import-export restrictions between U.S. and E.E.C.

References Available on request.

Sharon Flaherty
1250 Harvard Street N.W.
Washington, D.C. 20009
(202) 555-4119

Objective   To obtain a position as an assistant librarian where I can utilize my interpersonal and organizational skills.

Education

St. Anselms Academy, Washington, D.C., Class of 1998

Relevant Courses Taken:
*Business
*Office Systems
*Computers in Business
*Research Strategies
*English/Writing (four years)

Experience

Student Librarian, St. Anselms Academy, October 1996 - May 1998.

Responsibilities:

*Checked books out to students and teachers

*Maintained records of books on loan

*Checked returned books against borrowing records

*Advised students in the use of the card catalog

*Assisted users with computer database

*Answered questions about reference materials

*Maintained accurate shelving of books and periodicals

Special Skills and Achievements

*Experienced with on-line database references for library (use Reader's Guide to Periodical Literature, Business Periodicals Index, Science Periodicals Index, among others).

*Selected High School Student of the Month (March 1997) for ongoing volunteer activities with Stone Soup, and urban hunger project.

*Experienced with use of computers for word processing, page layout, and database management (WriteNow, WordPerfect, Print Shop, and Microsoft Works).

*Listed on Honor Roll each year; member of National Honor Society.

References are available at your request.

Claire Renard

618 N.W. Eighth Street, No. 215
Boca Raton, Florida 33486
Telephone: 561-555-1400

Objective
To obtain a position that will lead to a career in banking, where my skills in finance, accounting, and organization can be utilized effectively.

Education
Boca Raton High School, 1501 N.W. Fifteenth Street. Class of 1998.

Pertinent Courses: Business I and II, Economics, Accounting I and II, Business Writing, Office Management Systems, Typing I and II.

Achievements
Elected Student Body Treasurer. Chaired Finance Committee. Maintained student account books. Recorded income from student fund drives and disbursements for student charities and activities, 1997-1998.

Served on the Finance Committee for the Student Government, 1996-1997.

Coordinated Student Fund Drive which raised 20 percent more than the previous year's drive to benefit children's programs in Palm Beach County. Served as liaison with local community service center for direction of funds disbursement, 1996-1997.

Acted as Committee Representative to Student Body Executive Board. Attended meetings and presented financial reports to student body officers and advisors, 1996-1997.

Elected President of Business Club. Coordinated monthly meetings. Supervised planning for Business Career Day, 1997-1998.

Served as Treasurer of the Debate Club. Maintained records of dues and expenses for field trips and school visitations, 1995-1996.

Working knowledge of French. Completed four years of high school French and spent one month living in Quebec as part of an intensive language program.

Other Activities
Member of National Honor Society, Girls' Cross Country Track Team, Social Committee, Club Francais, Homecoming Committee

References
Available on request

Gretchen Morrison
2506 Chelsea Street
Tampa, Florida 33603
813-555-8220
Morris@aol.com

Objective   Entry-level position that will lead to a career in social service

Education   Temple Heights Christian School, Tampa
                   Graduation date: May 1999

                   Relevant Coursework: Human Development, Education, Social Science, Public
                   Government, Civics, Speech Communication

Experience   Volunteer Coordinator, Project Second Wind, Tampa Central District, 1998

                   Duties: Coordinated volunteers from five Tampa high schools. Planned strategies
                   for publicity, volunteer solicitation, site coordination, and area canvassing. Plotted
                   maps for canvassing communities. Worked with National Guard dispatch office to
                   coordinate drivers for collecting food donations through canvassing. On day of
                   drive, supervised canvassing efforts for the five areas. Coordinated delivery to
                   central warehouse.

                   Volunteer, Meals on Wheels, Tampa, 1995-1996

                   Duties: Prepared individual meal servings for weekly delivery to invalids in Tampa
                   area. Delivered meals and visited with invalids.

                   Counselor, Summer Camp, Tampa Heights Christian School, 1996-1998

                   Duties: Assumed responsibility for twelve girls aged 8 to 12. Prepared and
                   presented lessons in Bible study and environmentalism. Taught canoeing.
                   Provided guitar accompaniment for camp sing-alongs.

Activities   Active member of Say No club, which sponsored drug awareness programs at local
                   elementary schools.
                   Worked with student committees to plan social events.
                   Helped with publicity for student elections.
                   Played on softball team sponsored by local business.

References   Available on request.

Jameson W. Brussard, Jr.
212 N. Jefferson Street
Albany, Georgia 31701
(912) 555-2239

Objective   A position in customer service leading to a career in business management.

Sales Experience

Served as salesperson in sporting goods store. Over six-month period, made consistent increases in sales, which led to my being selected as salesperson of the quarter, spring 1998.

Sold compact discs and cassettes for a music store. Maintained position among top ten salespeople. Became very knowledgeable about both classical and contemporary music.

Leadership

Elected Senior Class Vice President, 1997-1998. Responsible for overseeing committees and served as senior class representative to Student Senate. Assumed responsibilities of class president in her absence.

Revived Business Club; served as president, 1997-1998. Set meeting agendas, presided over meetings, instituted fund drive to sponsor professional visits and field trips, organized trips to local business organizations.

Management

Managed Student Store, Monroe High School, 1996-1998. Supervised student clerks, scheduled work shifts, ordered supplies, received shipments and checked them against purchase orders, served customers.

Serve as Weekend Night Manager at a 125-room motel, July 1998-present. Greet guests, manage registration desk, supervise night staff, and serve as security representative on alternating weekends.

Work History

Weekend Night Manager, Motel Orleans, Albany, Georgia, July 1998-present
Salesperson, Jerfferson's Sporting Goods, Albany, Georgia, May 1997-June 1998
Salesperson, Musicland, Albany, Georgia, June 1995-May 1997

Education

Monroe High School, Albany, Georgia
Graduation class of 1998

Activities & Memberships: Business Club, Forensics Club, National Honor Society, Pep Club, Publicity Committee, Photography Club, JV and Varsity Wrestling.

References

Available on request.

SAMUEL JUN-LAN CHEN
2110 Cottage Grove Avenue
Chicago Heights, IL 60411
Telephone: 847-555-2645

OBJECTIVE   To obtain a laboratory research assistant position in a scientific lab.

EDUCATION   Bloom High School, 101 West Tenth Street, Chicago Heights, Illinois
Graduated with highest honors, 1998. Cumulative G.P.A.: 3.96

RELEVANT COURSES TAKEN:
*Biology (two years)
*General Chemistry (one year)
*Organic Chemistry (one year)
*Physics (one year)
*Botany (one semester)
*Math (algebra, trigonometry, calculus)

EXPERIENCE   Laboratory Assistant, Bloom High School, Chemistry Section, 1997-1998
*Assisted teacher with laboratory preparation and set-up
*Answered student questions about laboratory experiments
*Graded lab worksheets and recorded grades for chemistry teacher
*Maintained chemical stockroom and kept track of supplies

Laboratory Assistant, Bloom High School, Biology Section, 1996-1997
*Assisted with laboratory preparation and clean-up
*Worked with students on dissection projects (frog, fetal pig heart)
*Graded student lab worksheets
*Installed and tested new computer software for simulated dissection
*Directed students in use of computer software

ACTIVITIES   *Member, Future Scientists of America
*Secretary, Bloom High Science Club
*Coordinated visitation day for seven scientists from Chicago-area research
 institutions and manufacturing companies
*Served as general science assistant for science teachers

REFERENCES   Available on request.

STEWART SULLIVAN

OBJECTIVE   To secure a position on the production staff of a printing company where I can utilize my skills with graphic design and layout.

EXPERIENCE   Graphic Artist, Student Yearbook Staff, 1996-1998

Assumed responsibility for overall design concepts in 212-page hardbound yearbook.

Provided design assistance to editorial staff. Developed graphic elements for pages needing artwork.

Designed page layouts.

Mastered computer page-layout technology and desktop publishing software.

Prepared photographs for publication (cropped, sized).

Supervised staff of production assistants.

Production Assistant, Borah Gazette, 1995-1997

Prepared layout for student newspaper.

Cropped, sized, and positioned photographs.

Designed graphics to accent advertisement section.

EDUCATION   Borah Senior High School, Boise, Idaho
Class of 1999. Grade point average in art: 4.0.

Areas of study: journalism, photojournalism, graphic design, art (painting, drawing, watercolor, ceramics).

REFERENCES   Available on request.

1220 North Cole Road ~ Boise, Idaho 83709 ~ 208-555-2477

PETER PERKINS

601 E. Allis Drive
Milwaukee, WI 53201
414/555-1133

OBJECTIVE: A career in the manufacturing field.

EDUCATION: **Milwaukee Vocational High School,** Milwaukee, Wisconsin
Degree Expected: June 1999

Course work:

Manufacturing Design	Wood Shop
Welding	Drafting
Technical Writing	Auto Shop

**WORK
HISTORY:** **Wisconsin Manufacturing Company,** Milwaukee, Wisconsin
Forklift Driver, Summers, 1997, 1998

Drove forklifts. Repaired and serviced heavy machinery.

Penner Furniture, Inc., West Allis, Wisconsin
Warehouse Assistant, 1995-1997

Prepared furniture for delivery. Organized furniture stock. Delivered furniture.
Assisted in construction of furniture racks.

REFERENCES AVAILABLE

Joanna C. Harper
1150 S. 16th Street
Decatur, Illinois 62521
847-555-2366

Job Sought   Word processing operator, full-time summer employment.

Education
and Training   MacArthur High School, Decatur, Illinois   Graduation: June 1999

My major area of emphasis has been business, with course work in office
procedures, business machines, business communications, keyboarding
(beginning and advanced), computer applications, and accounting.

Specific training includes computer graphics, word processing, data
processing, and electronic spreadsheet. I have also received some
basic instruction in desktop publishing. My word processing speed is
65 words per minute, and I operate a 10-key adding machine at approximately
35 numbers per minute.

Work
Experience   James Brophy, D.D.S.   Summer 1997
1267 S. 15th Street, Decatur, Illinois 62521   847-555-0112
Supervisor: Mrs. Dionne Avery

Job duties: assisted with word processing, filing, typing, answering telephones,
scheduling appointments, and managing the reception desk.

Mr. Arva Ellison
7878 S. Cantrell Street, Decatur, Illinois 65251   1992-1997

Job duties: provided child care for three children, part-time throughout the
school year and full-time during the summer.

Ellison Farms
988 Meadow Road, Decatur, Illinois 65251   Summer 1994 and 1995

Job duties: operated seeder, assisted with harvest of a variety of crops, assisted
with irrigation systems, and provided general labor.

Activities   Varsity Rally Squad: Basketball
Played flute in Concert Band
Recreational Cross-Country Ski Club
Drama Club

References   Available on request

_____

Parker Adams
226 N. Fifth Street, Apt. 42
Fairbury, Illinois 61739
Telephone: 815-555-1154

Position Desired:

Full-time summer employment that makes use of my background as a lab assistant and agricultural worker. My long-term career goal is to become a biomedical engineer.

Education and Training:

Prarie Central High School, Fairbury, Illinois.   Graduation anticipated: June 1999

My major area of emphasis has been science. During the past three years, I have completed all of the science courses offered at PCHS, including Biology, Chemistry, Anatomy and Physiology, Physics, Earth Science, Field Biology, Horticulture, and Advanced Chemistry. I have participated in extra-credit research projects in most of these courses. Science grade point average: 3.68.

Experience:

Organization:	As a lab assistant in the science program, I have organized labs, maintained inventory of supplies, entered data into the computer, and assisted students with class assignments.
Equipment:	I have operated microscopes, digital meters, and oscilloscopes. I also drive a tractor when working on my grandfather's seed farm.
Efficiency:	During my junior year, I worked as a laborer on the family farm approximately 20 hours per week. I was concurrently working on a special honors science project which required several hours each week of after-school study. I was able to manage my time efficiently and maintain a 3.9 grade point average for the year.

Honors:

First Place Project Award, Science VII, Regional Skills Conference, 1998
Honorable Mention, Science VI, Regional Skills Conference, 1997

References are available upon request.

Laura Chen
5527 N.W. Oak Creek Road
Ashland, Oregon 97520
(503) 555-9982

Job Sought: Entry-level position in the field of environmental economics.

Education & Training:

Mt. Ashland Senior High School, Ashland, Oregon 97520
Graduation Class of 1998
Cumulative G.P.A.: 3.95

Science & Math Courses:
*Earth Science
*Horticulture
*Biology
*Algebra 1 & 2
*Probability & Statistics

Business and Economics Courses:
*Business Communications
*Economics & Government
*Capstone Economics
*Computer Applications
*Computer Keyboarding

Work Experience:

Prudential Bache Securities   Internship, Summer 1997
One Union Square, Suite 2400, Seattle, Washington 98122
Supervisor: Kathryn Mix, (205) 555-9111

Duties: Posted account records in ledger and conducted research on major corporations.
Major area of interest was product liability suits against corporations filing Chapter 11 to
escape same suit.

Brown's Steak House   October 1996 to present
17 First Street, Ashland, Oregon 97520
Supervisor: Joseph Brown, (503) 555-2219

Duties: Hostess in charge of seating clients at the restaurant during peak evening hours.
Manage cashier's station. Work part-time while going to school.

Oregon River Experience   Summer 1994 to present
34497 Tall Pines Drive, Grants Pass, Oregon 97526
Supervisor: John Hendersen (503) 555-2294

Duties: From May to October (with the exception of 1997) I have worked either as a lead
guide or a support guide. As a lead guide, I lead raft trips down the Rogue River, organize
equipment and travel logistics, plan and cook menus, and am responsible for knowledge of
the river and surrounding area as well as for the safety and equipment of a group of 25 to 30
people for two to five days. As a support guide, I assist the lead guide in carrying out these
responsibilities and row the supply boat.

REFERENCES AVAILABLE

Patrick O'Callahan
1806 N. Washington Avenue, Apartment 362
Evansville, Indiana 47711-2298
Telephone: (812) 555-2295
Message: (812) 555-2983

Objective	Career in business administration management.

Education   North High School, Evansville, Indiana   Graduating Class of 1999

My course program has centered on a business and management curriculum. Specific courses include Business Law, Business Management, Economics, Accounting, Leadership, Public Speaking, Psychology, Sociology, Personal Relationships, and Japanese. My grade point average in these areas is 3.83.

Communication Skills

Completed three years of language arts courses, including Advanced Composition and Business Communications.

Arranged and directed student discussion panel on global issues.

Interacted successfully with the public in positions as a sales representative and a part-time waiter.

Served as campaign coordinator for successful student body presidential candidate.

Participated in debate team and forensics squad. Won two regional first-place awards in debate and three second-place awards in persuasive speaking.

Leadership Skills

Served two terms as student president for Junior Achievement. During that time membership increased 23 percent, and our organization was named best in the state. Established subcommittees to target membership drives and continue organizational development.

Served as treasurer of Future Business Leaders of America, Evansville Regional Chapter. Coordinated joint activities among Bosse, Central, Harrison, North, and Reitz high schools. Coordinated business career fair at city convention center. Worked with committee chairs to coordinate school visitations to promote business to junior high schools.

Experience   Sales Representative   Summers 1996-1998
Prange's Department Store, Boys Sportswear
Supervisor: Joey Ableman

Waiter   May 1995-June 1996
The Fish House
Supervisor: Annette Townsend

References   Available on request.

Dylan James McDonald
1415 Wenig Road N.E.
Cedar Rapids, Iowa 52402
(319) 555-2284

Occupational Objective

To obtain an entry-level position with a computer software manufacturer where my skills in computer programming and applications might lead to advancement in program design.

Educational Background

Metro High School, Cedar Rapids, Iowa   Current Status: Senior
Computer Science G.P.A.: 4.0   Cumulative G.P.A.: 3.66

Computer Expertise

Completed three semesters of computer programming.
Developed programming projects individually and in teams.
Proficient in BASIC, PASCAL, and Hypercard programming languages.
Initiated self-study FORTRAN program project.
Familiar with word processing, spreadsheet, and database programs.
Knowledge of desktop publishing and graphic design software.
Highly experienced with MS DOS operating platforms.
Basic knowledge of UNIX-based systems.
Worked on special three-month project using NEXT computer system.

Work History

Administrative Assistant, Health Care Nursing Center, Cedar Rapids
June 1996 to present

Serve as swing shift assistant manager for 60-bed facility. Supervise maintenance personnel. Also responsible for some support services, including patient form processing, database management, record-keeping, and filing.

Young Men's Christian Association, Cedar Rapids
September 1995 to June 1996

Supervised various evening recreational activities in facility that included swimming pool, shuffleboard, Ping-Pong, bowling lanes, and a gymnasium. Responsible for equipment check-out and locker room inspections.

Extracurricular Activities

Vice President, Keyboard Club (member since 1995; V.P. 1996-1997)
Peer tutor, mathematics
Student Empowerment Training Project (STEP) Leadership Training

Honors

YMCA Youth of the Month, June 1996
Computer Programming Award, Science VII Regional Competition
National Honor Society Scholar of the Month, May 1997

References

Available on request.

Asher Toppman
10220 Goodwood Boulevard
Baton Rouge, Louisiana 70802
(504) 555-8820

Career Objective	To become an efficient and effective legal assistant while beginning preparations for entering college pre-law program.
Education	Broadmoor High School, Baton Rouge, Louisiana Current status: Senior Current G.P.A.: 3.98
Leadership	President, Associated Student Body of Broadmoor High School, 1997-1998
	Junior Class President, BHS, 1996-1997
	Sophomore Class Vice President, BHS, 1996-1997
	Freshman Student Senate Representative, Social Studies, 1995-1996
	President, Forensis Team, 1995-1996
	News Director, Radio Club, 1996-1997
Communication	Completed six semesters in writing and communication courses.
	Presented numerous speeches in forensics competition.
	Presented campaign speeches for elected offices.
	Won Young Democrats of America essay contest, 1998.
	Completed exploratory honors project in radio broadcasting.
	Served as news director for weekly 15-minute radio show on WBTR, produced by radio club.
Organization	Directed planning and execution of several student events while serving as student body president and junior class president.
	Served on student senate ethics committee, which sponsored Honor Day and a "drug-free zone" day.
	Developed editorial procedures for planning weekly news broadcasts with other radio club officers.
Honors	Kiwanis Club Scholarship Designee, 1997
	Honors Program, Best Project Award, 1996
	Merit Scholar, Broadmoor PTA, 1995-1997

References are available on request

Tristan Swanson
19 Malta Street
Augusta, Maine 04330

Objective

A career in media communications where my writing and
editorial skills will be utilized to advantage.

Education

Cony High School, Augusta, Maine   Anticipated Graduation: May 1999
Major Area of Study: Journalism and Communications

Writing Experience

- Activities and Entertainment Editor, *Cony Crier*, student newspaper, junior year.
- Wrote monthly column for local city newspaper, *Kennebec Journal*, High School page.
- Worked as reporter for the *Cony Crier* since freshman year.
- Completed two years of specialized course work in journalism and media communications.
- Wrote script for documentary film on ocean pollution on the Eastern Seaboard.
- Won publication of two poems in National Young Poets '97 competition, Boston, Mass.

Leadership Experience

- Served as social committee chairman for student body of Cony High School. Planned various social events such as dances, barbecues, pep rallies, and a speaker's forum.

- Active in Letterman's Club, a service club of varsity sports players. Organized food drives and raffle to benefit Hunger Project.

- Captain, Varsity Basketball Team. Responsible for encouraging players in pre-game and post-practice activities.

Work History

- Bath Cove Fleet, Bath, Maine. Worked on a fishing boat as cook's helper and crew member. Summers, 1996-1998.

- Burger King, Augusta, Maine. Worked part-time as kitchen staff and line cook while attending school. September 1997-May 1998.

References are available on request.

Allison Barnes
2880 West Braddock Road
Alexandria, Virginia 22302
Telephone: 703-555-1283

Career Objective   To obtain a position with a small theater company where my background in theater will allow me to make contributions in a variety of areas.

Experience   Directed production of Arthur Miller's *Death of a Salesman*. Took play to state drama competition and received honorable mention.

Played Lisl in Community Theatre production of *The Sound of Music*. Won the part from among 84 auditioners.

Designed sets and costumes, and worked on costume and set building crews, for a production of Shakespeare's *Twelfth Night*.

Sang the lead in *Oklahoma*.

Played a walk-on part in *Our Town*. Served backstage as key grip.

Assisted with design and production of lighting for *Faculty Follies*, an entirely student-directed production starring teachers, counselors, and administrators from throughout the high school.

Operated video cameras during dress rehearsals for *Our Town* and *Twelfth Night*.

Wrote reviews of local theater (non-school) productions for student newspaper. One review was published in the weekend edition of the *Alexandria Gazette*.

Education   Williams Senior High School, Alexandria, Virginia, Class of 1999

Courses: Drama, Advanced Drama, Play Writing, Special Projects: Theater, Shakespeare, Creative Writing, Advanced Composition, and Journalism

Work History   Waitress, New Morning Cafe, Alexandria
January 1996 - present

References   Available on request.

SUZANNE BARSTOW
2248 W. Billtown Road, Apt. 16
Louisville, Kentucky 40215
502/555-7751

JOB OBJECTIVE

A part-time position as nurse's assistant in a hospital or health care facility. My long-term career goal is to become a pediatrician.

EXPERIENCE

Candy Striper, Louisville General Hospital   Volunteer 1995-present

Duties: Assist nurses with distribution of medication, visit with patients, deliver reading materials and other items at patient's request, provide general assistance to nursing staff.

EDUCATION

Iriquois High School, Taylor Boulevard, Louisville   Class of 1999
Major course of study: Health and Physical Education   Current G.P.A.: 3.89

Courses Completed: Anatomy and Physiology, Basic Health, Personal Health: Wellness, CPR-First Aid, Childhood Development, Advanced Foods and Nutrition.

COMMUNICATION SKILLS

Completed three semesters of courses that specialized in written and oral business communication.

Served as school spirit committee chair. Built sense of school spirit by establishing pep section for all athletic events. Coordinated with school band and rally squads to encourage participation.

Participated for two semesters in forensics, presenting a variety of speeches on topics ranging from personal health and fitness to political issues.

INTERPERSONAL SKILLS

Attentive listener, able to lend a sympathetic, nonjudgmental ear when needed.

Able to gain trust and rapport with various types of individuals.

Concerned and empathetic, willing to help those in need.

HONORS

Member of the National Honor Society

Selected Candy Striper of the Month, Louisville General Hospital

Placed second in state forensics competition, exposition category

REFERENCES AVAILABLE ON REQUEST

Joshua Whitely
228 West Fifth Street
P.O. Box 286
Emporia, Kansas 66801
316-555-2251

Job Sought	Full-time summer position with manufacturing company or warehouse.
Education	Emporia High School, Emporia, Kansas Class of 1999
Experience	Jayhawk Auto Parts, Emporia Clerk, Summers 1996 and 1997 *Duties:* Serve customers, answer questions about auto parts and other merchandise, maintain order in stockroom, find parts by order number on stock shelves, remove items sold from computer inventory, assist with receiving shipments and entering new stock in computer inventory.
Activities	Varsity and junior varsity sports: football, basketball, baseball, Freshman football, cross country Key Club Spirit Club
References	Available on request

McHale Newport
2200 River Road, No. 126
Annapolis, Maryland 21401
301/555-8461

Professional Goal

To obtain an entry-level position in the news department of a daily newspaper where I can utilize my journalistic skills and professionalism.

Education

Broadneck Senior High School
1265 Green Holly Drive, Annapolis, Maryland
Class of 1999

Writing Experience

Student Reporter, The BSHS Times, Broadneck High School, 1995-present

Wrote articles on student government, administrative decisions, school board meetings, student activities, sports events, and profiles of student leaders and teachers. Entered copy on computer word processing software. Served one semester as interim editor, determined story assignments for student reporters, worked with advisor on writing editorials, and edited news copy submitted by student reporters. Served as staff photographer on several occasions.

Freelance Writer, 1997 to present

Published two articles in the "Teen Beat" section of the *Capitol* (Annapolis daily newspaper). Published one personality profile of the high school principal in *American Teen* magazine. Submitted several query letters and manuscripts to a variety of magazines for publication.

Activities

Junior Press Club of Annapolis (a local high school division of the Maryland Press Club)
The Lancer, Broadneck SHS student annual (helped with photography, layout, editing)
Aperture (photography club)

References and portfolio of writing and photography are available on request.

Mary Alice Simpson
1280 Delaware Avenue, Apt. 116
Buffalo, New York 24214
716/555-8482

Objective

I am seeking an internship with a business enterprise where my skills in writing and communication may contribute to the effectiveness of the organization.

Education

Holy Angels Academy, 24 Shoshane Street, Buffalo, New York 14214
Class of 1999
Cumulative Grade Point Average: 3.38

Course of Study

My high school curriculum has offered me a broad background in liberal studies and business in preparation for attending college. In addition to course work in business, management, and accounting, I participated in the college preparatory honors program, which offered intensive courses in U.S. and European History, English Composition, Research Methods, and Social Studies.

Achievements and Activities

Selected to serve as senior monitor for academic testing programs.

Served on student government committee for finance. Conducted several successful campaigns to raise funds for school programs.

Participated in the a capella choir, madrigal singers, and concert choir.

Assisted with parent night preparations and planning.

Member of the *Quill* staff, which published a school literary magazine.

Published three poems in *Quill.*

References are available on request.

Tamar Su Sutterby
2404 Gallant Road
Charlotte, NC 28216
(704) 555-2119

Objective   To obtain a position as a receptionist or clerical specialist.

Education   Central High School, Charlotte, North Carolina
Graduation date: June 1992

Courses taken:
Keyboarding Skill Building (65 w.p.m.)
Computer Applications
Business Machines
Word Processing, WordPerfect
Office Systems
Business Communications

Experience   **Clerical Assistant,** Central High School, Charlotte, January-March 1998
Worked with office staff as part of cooperative work experience program for class credit. Enhanced office and business skills through on-the-job learning. Duties included filing, typing, answering telephones, and serving as front desk receptionist.

Cashier, Wendy's Restaurant, Charlotte, June-August 1997
Worked front line cashier station nd drive-through window. Greeted customers, collected prepared food according to orders, handled money, balanced cash drawer.

Activities   Ski Club, Young Republicans of North Carolina, Pep Club, Varsity Wrestling, Rally, Drama Club, Girls Choir

References   Available on request.

Robin Weiss
2250 Second Avenue
Akron, Ohio 44313
Telephone: 216-555-9941

JOB SOUGHT	Salesclerk with sporting goods or department store.
EDUCATION	Firestone High School, Akron, Ohio Class of 1999
EXPERIENCE	Salesclerk, Firestone Student Store, 9/98-present. Operated student store sales. Handled cash exchanges and credit account charges. Balanced daily receipts. Referee, Summit County Soccer Clubs, 1995-1997. Served as referee for elementary and junior high school-level soccer games.
SPECIAL SKILLS	Trained in CPR and advanced lifesaving. Knowledgeable about a wide variety of outdoor sports.
ACTIVITIES	Recreational Water Sports Club Outdoor School Counselor Explorers Club
REFERENCES	Available on request

Brenda Pitt-Williams

3488 Chester Avenue
Philadelphia, Pennsylvania 19151
Messages: 215/555-7741

Objective	Nurse's Aide in health care organization.
Education	Friends Central School North 68th and City Avenue Philadelphia, PA 19151 Graduate, 1998
Abilities	Trained in CPR and emergency first aid. Experienced in working with invalids. Completed coursework in human anatomy and physiology. Studied nutrition and stress management. Worked with children involved in crisis intervention. Experienced in maintaining antiseptic environment.
Experience	Volunteer, Cheltenham Nursing Home, 1996 to present. Visit with elderly invalids. Read letters and newspapers to those who need assistance. Help maintenance staff with maintaining cleanliness. Assist nursing staff with rounds and distribution of food trays. Volunteer, Women's Shelter, operated by the Friends Society, 1995 to 1997. Helped children of women staying at the shelter adjust to changes. Gathered donations of toys and games and played with children of all ages. Baby-sitter, various private individuals, 1992 to present. Provide child care for several children, from three months to twelve years of age. Have cared for as many as seven children at a time.
Activities	Scholarship and Leadership Committee Volunteer Assistance League Friends for Peaceful Conflict Resolution, Junior Chapter Study Session Leader Peer Tutor, English and history

References are available upon request.

Burke Anderson

260 E. North Avenue
Baltimore, Maryland 21202
301/555-4458

Objective   A career in technology design and development that will utilize my skills
in technology innovation and traditional and computer-aided drafting.

Education   Baltimore City High School, Baltimore, Maryland
Major area of study: science and technology
G.P.A. in major: 6.0 (scale of six); cumulative G.P.A.: 4.85

Accomplishments

Tied for Best of Show in regional competition, Technology Challenge '98,
held at Massachusetts Institute of Technology, for the design and
construction of a hovercraft.

Qualified for competition in Technology Challenge '97 with the design and
construction of a solar-powered remote-controlled sailboat.

Completed the following course work, maintaining a 6.0 grade point average:

Drafting 1-4	Metal Technology
Electricity/Electronics	Wood Technology
Computer-Aided Drafting	Design and Technology 1-2
Career Mechanics	

Participated in Cooperative Work Experience projects in drafting and career
mechanics.

Work Experience

Drafting Intern, Cardell Associates, Baltimore, Maryland, Summer 1998.
Duties: Checked blueprints of CAD-drafted plans for parts and equipment
manufactured by Cardell. Drafted initial drawings of existing parts that required
changes to fit new machinery.

Mechanics Intern, East Baltimore Auto, Baltimore, Maryland, Summer 1997.
Duties: Worked as assistant mechanic for import cars. Learned diagnostics
procedures and equipment operation.

Activities   Techies, BCHS technology club
Young Sailors of Baltimore
Radio Club

References and portfolio of drafting projects available on request.

Bruce C. Cantrell
120 Border Street
Hot Springs, Arkansas 71901
Telephone: 501/555-7367

OBJECTIVE

Summer internship with company doing business with international import and export trade.

EDUCATION

Lakeside Senior High School, Malvern Road, Hot Springs, Arkansas
Graduation date: 1998. Major: Business.

Specialized Courses: business series courses in accounting and management, marketing, Japanese I and II, Economics, Introduction to Statistics.
Current G.P.A.: 3.9.

Special Projects: Developed three-year business finance, development and marketing plan for simulated business. In economics, made most significant profit margin from series of planned investments.

WORK EXPERIENCE

Garland County Exposition Center, Hot Springs, Arkansas   Work Crew
Supervisor: Morgan Stewart   5/98-9/98

Duties: Worked during summer exhibition season. Responsibilities included grounds maintenance, ticket selling, livestock herding and registration, and event preparation.

Sentinel-Record, Hot Springs, Arkansas   Newspaper Delivery
Supervisor: Walter E. Ballentine Jr.   9/92-5/97

Lakeside Senior High School   Grounds Crew
Supervisor: Connie Lofstedt

ACTIVITIES

Future Business Leaders of America, Hot Springs, Junior Achievement, Junior Class Treasurer, S Club (service honorary).

References are available on request.

Brittany Schoonover
318 S.E. 151st Street ~ Eugene, Oregon 97405 ~ (503) 555-6246

Education

South Eugene High School, Eugene, Oregon
Expected graduation date: 1999

Rex Putnam High School, 4950 S.E. Roethe Road, Milwaukee, Oregon 97267
1995-1996

Skills

*Typing (55 wpm)	*Strong writing skills
*Computer keyboarding (70 wpm)	*Business communications training
*Ten-key adding machine (40 wpm)	*Business systems training

Work Experience

*Data entry, State of Oregon Human Resources Division, Eugene, Oregon 97233
June-August 1998

Duties included transferring data from handwritten forms onto computer forms, checking data entries for accuracy and making needed corrections, and sorting and filing computer printouts.

Activities

*Peer tutor in language arts
*Rally squad, junior varsity basketball
*Social events program committee
*Library assistance league
*School literary magazine editorial committee

References

Available on request.

Melinda W. Adams
810 N. 1430 Del Rio Drive
Tempe, Arizona 85282
(503) 555-9530

Objective

Seeking summer employment in retail sales that will continue as part-time employment during the school year.

Education

Corona Del Sol High School. Expected graduation date: 1999.

Courses:
*computer applications
*word processing
*office management
*two years of math
*two years of business

Work Experience

Office Assistant, Dave Whitehead Insurance Company, Tempe. 9/96-present
Duties: answering telephones, assisting clients, answering questions about insurance claims, filling out claim forms, operating office machines, word processing, and filing.

Cashier and Hostess, Judie's Chicken Haven, Lakeshore Drive, Tempe. 6/96-9/96
Duties: greeting and seating customers, assisting waitresses and busboys with clearing and setting tables, entering sales in cash register, making change.

Achievements

*Volleyball and basketball team member; volleyball player of the year 1996
*First flute soloist, concert orchestra
*Jazz ensemble
*Drill team; served as captain 1996-1998
*Music Appreciation Club member

References

Available on request

KARIN BOWLES
2050 CROWN BOULEVARD, APT. C ~ DENVER, CO 80204 ~ (303)555-2280

GOAL   A career in business administration.

EXPERIENCE

LEADERSHIP   As a member of the finance committee for the Associated Students of
Kennedy High School, I was responsible for supervising the planning
and execution of school-wide fund-raising projects such as candy sales
and the student carnival. I also set meeting dates and presided over
meetings, reported to student council, and worked with the student
government advisor on budgeting.

COMMUNICATION   Worked on the publicity committees for several student events and
election campaigns. Wrote text for fliers and signs and assisted with
speech writing. Each campaign ended in election victory for my
candidate.

Completed two semesters of business communications courses. Also
completed three years of honors-level English composition and three
years of French. Have working knowledge of spoken and written
French.

ORGANIZATION   Served as assistant librarian, a position usually held by a paid
professional, during the semester prior to graduation. Directed a
research methods seminar for freshman students. Answered
questions about library reference materials and on-line research
sources. Supervised student workers in shelving books. Updated
computerized database.

EDUCATION   Kennedy High School
2855 S. Lamar Street
Denver, CO 80227
9/94-6/98
Final G.P.A.: 3.75

Pertinent Courses: Business Law, Accounting, Computer Applications
in Business, Office Procedures, Word Processing, Business
Management

REFERENCES   Available on request

Jennifer Smith 345 Forest Street, Dover, Delaware 19901
(302) 555-5835

Job Sought

Classroom assistant position in preschool, day care center, or elementary school.

Relevant Experience

Dover Elementary School
Supervisor: Mrs. Wilkerson

Duties: Worked for one semester as part of exploratory education experience class. Assisted kindergarten teacher with supervision of students on playground and during classroom activities. Read stories and directed group activities. Taught songs and rhythm.

Education

9/94 - 6/98   Dover High School, Walker Road, Dover, Delaware

9/91 - 6/94   Dover Air Force Base Middle School, Hawthorne Drive, Dover, Delaware

Related Coursework:

Exploring Childhood I and II, Human Development, First Aid and Safety, Basic Health

Work History

6/97-present   Clerk, Dover AFB Commissary. Assist with stocking and daily preparation.

References on request

Judith Fritch
16047 E. Bentsen, Apartment 25
Portland, Oregon 97223
(503) 555-5121

Objective	To obtain a part-time clerical job in a city or county government office where I can utilize my office management skills.
Skills	Professional attitude Organized 10-key adding machine Reliable Typing 60 wpm Responsible Word processing 75 wpm Self-starter Filing Motivated for success
Education	I am currently a senior at Central High School, Bay City, Oregon, with an expected graduation date of June 1999. Graduation seminar project: currently involved in preparing an in-depth report on business management systems and operations in city and county government offices.
Experience	Receptionist Thrifty Auto Leasing, 456 Central Boulevard, Bay City July 1996 - January 1998 Duties: Managed telephone switchboard, assisted clients, directed clients to appropriate department, typed letters, typed auto leasing forms, filed, assisted sales staff. References available on request

<u>Kenneth Zimmerman</u>
Route 32, Box 2216
Central Valley, New York 10917
(914) 555-4481

<u>Objective</u>

A position with a political action organization working for social improvement.

<u>Education</u>

Monroe-Woodbury High School, Central Valley, NY
Anticipated graduation date: 1999.

<u>Skills & Achievements</u>

*Experienced with a variety of computer software and hardware, including Word and Works on Mac and IBM.

*Experienced with providing customer service.

*Trained in basic bookkeeping, invoicing, inventory, and payroll procedures.

*Effective leadership skills: served as vice president of Associated Students of Monroe-Woodbury High School, founder and president of Students for Global Awareness, director of one-act play for student drama presentation.

*Excellent writing and communications skills. Wrote and presented several speeches during all-school election campaign. Ran on platform of working to improve student awareness of global issues.

<u>Employment History</u>

Sales Assistant, Video Circle, Chester, NY. June-Sept. 1997.
     Duties: Provide assistance to customers in video sales and rental store. Worked with database on IBM-compatible computer system. Handled cash and credit card transactions. Maintained accurate inventory system.

References available on request.

Mary Jo Azukas
14 West 22nd Street
Trenton, NJ 08602
(609) 555-3477

Objective

To obtain a position as assistant manager in a small restaurant.

Experience

Head Cashier, <u>Burgerville USA</u>, Trenton, September 1997-present

<u>Duties</u>: Supervise cashier staff during evening shift. Check balance sheets at end of shift. Work counter and drive-through window as needed.

Line Cook/Cashier, <u>Tony's Burger Emporium</u>, Trenton, June 1996 - August 1997

<u>Duties</u>: Greeted customers, took orders, helped kitchen crew prepare meals and drinks, assisted with maintaining stock, cleaning, and closing procedures. Responsible for having balanced till after each shift.

Education

Capitol High School, Trenton
Class of 1999

Honors

Cashier of the Month, <u>Burgerville USA</u>, February 1998
Junior Cheerleader of the Year, 1998
"Cappy" Award for best supporting actress in a student production, 1998

References are available on request.

ANTOINETTE RUPERT
238 Orange Street
Tampa, FL 33606
(813) 555-3953

OBJECTIVE

To become part of the support services team for a small but growing business.

EDUCATION

Tampa Central High School, 480 Sherman Parkway, New Haven. Diploma, June 1998.

Concentration: Accounting I and II, Computer Applications I and II (word processing, spreadsheet, database, design, page layout and communications software for MS DOS operating platforms), Business Management, and Business Communications.

EXPERIENCE

Temporary Clerical Worker. Kelly Services, 1997-present

Duties: Worked for a wide range of clients, including a bank, mortgage trust company, supply warehouse, architectural office, city government office, and law office. Duties included typing, filing, answering telephones, preparing forms, computer data entry, transcribing dictation, and general office assistance.

ACTIVITIES & ACHIEVEMENTS

Secretary, Junior Class TCHS, 1997-1998
Assistant Editor, TCHS Yearbook, 1996-1997
Secretary, Future Business Leaders of America, 1995-1996
Member, Student Recycling Committee, 1997-1998
Member, TCHS Camera Club, 1996-1998

References are available on request

PAUL JEROME
412 Lincoln
Las Vegas, Nevada 87701
505-555-6623

OBJECTIVE   Seeking summer employment on the restaurant staff of a large hotel. Long-term goal: a career in hotel and restaurant management.

EDUCATION   South High School, 300 Chesterfield Avenue, Las Vegas, Class of 1999.

EXPERIENCE   Grounds Crew, Circus Circus, Las Vegas. June-August 1998.

~Duties: Trimmed hedges, replaced indoor and outdoor plants, operated irrigation system, kept walkways and grounds clean, assisted with pool maintenance.

Busboy, Denny's Restaurant, Las Vegas. September 1997-June 1998.

~Duties: Assisted waitresses with serving meals, cleared and set tables, served beverages.

Maintenance Crew, Caesar's Palace, Las Vegas. June-August 1997.

~Duties: Maintained regular schedule of pool maintenance, assisted with janitorial responsibilities, worked with grounds crew on landscape maintenance, provided some assistance with equipment repair.

REFERENCES AVAILABLE

Tony Pomeroy
2307 N. Broad Street
Philadelphia, PA 19119
(215) 555-2258

OBJECTIVE

A staff position as a photographer or darkroom technician on a newspaper or magazine.

EDUCATION

Northeast Prep School, Cottman Avenue, Philadelphia. Class of 1998.

Course emphases: Journalism, Photojournalism, Photography 1-3, Darkroom (beginning and advanced), Computer Applications in Art.

RELEVANT SKILLS & EXPERIENCE

Completed projects in three fields: black-and-white 35-mm photography, photo silkscreen and offset printing, and computer alteration of photographic imagery (using Digital Darkroom on Macintosh computer).

Won first place in *Philadelphia Daily News* amateur photo contest, high school category. Photo published in July 1998 edition.

Completed photo essay for submission to regional amateur photo contest sponsored by Kodak. (Results as yet undetermined.)

Operated copy camera for making PMTs and halftone screens.

Completed extracurricular project on 35mm color photography.

WORK HISTORY

Northeast Prep Student Newspaper
Photo Editor, 1997-1998
Staff Photographer, 1994-1996

Supervised student photography staff. Selected photographs for publication from analysis of negative or contact sheets. Assigned photography projects and maintained check-out of school cameras. Shot, developed, and printed photographs.

EXTRACURRICULAR ACTIVITIES

Camera Club, President
Brush and Easel (art student association)

PORTFOLIO AND REFERENCES AVAILABLE UPON REQUEST

Timothy J. Davison
1286 West Shore Road, Apt. 5
Warwick, Rhode Island 02889
Telephone: 402-555-2117

Objective

A position as chef's assistant at a restaurant featuring specialty or gourmet cuisine.

Education

The Culinary Institute
114 First Avenue
New York, NY 10019
Video correspondence course, to be completed December 1998.

Taft Senior High School
575 Centerville Road
Warwick, RI 02886
Class standing: Junior

Special Skills

- Worked with International Student Club to plan and prepare a meal for 250 parents and students. Involved with menu planning and food preparation for dishes from all over the world.

- Catered a dinner party for six people as part of a donation of services to fund-raise for local Boys and Girls Club. Prepared and helped serve five-course dinner.

- Completed one year of culinary video correspondence course that involved preparation of primarily French cuisine. Although not required by course, I have followed a procedure of preparing the lesson plan menu for a group of four to six people who provide a written evaluation of the meal and its presentation.

- Completed two years of high school food preparation courses, including experience with food decoration.

Work Experience

Kitchen Prep Staff, June 1997-present
Warwick Towers Restaurant
34 Warwick Lake Avenue
Warwick, RI 02889

References are available on request.

Toby Waterson
200 South Third Avenue
Arcadia, California 91006
213-555-9226

Objective	A position with the technical department of a manufacturing company.
Experience	**Technical Design**
	*Designed and built solar-powered car (one-person).
	*Designed multi-media computer-directed light and sound presentation.
	*Developed model for automated, solar-powered home.
	*Completed two years of design and technology program.
	Engine Mechanics
	*Built motor for solar-powered car.
	*Assisted with engine rebuilding on two Volkswagens.
	*Assisted in engine repair on riding and other lawn mowers.
Work History	Grounds Crew/Maintenance, June 1997-present
	Riverview Apartments
	Arcadia, California
	*Duties: landscape maintenance, some plumbing, carpentry, general repair.
	Library Assistant, 1996-1997
	Foothills Junior High School
	Arcadia California
	*Duties: audio-visual equipment repair, office work, reshelving, data entry.
Education	Arcadia Senior High School, Class of 1998
	Major: Design and Technology
References	Available on request

Jasmine Parker
4223 Kilauea Avenue
P.O. Box 2214
Honolulu, Hawaii 96819
Phone: 818-555-2294

Objective

To obtain a position in fisheries and wildlife management administration that will utilize my skills in scientific research, analysis, and communication.

Education

Honolulu Community College, Dillingham Boulevard, Honolulu.
Enrolled in summer open enrollment programs, 1997 and 1998.
Earned 3.6 G.P.A. in science courses.

Kaimuki High School, 2705 Kaimuka Avenue, Honolulu.
Graduate 1998. Science G.P.A.: 4.0. Cumulative G.P.A.: 3.56

Science Background

Designed and conducted research project on underwater testing procedures

Assisted with research project designed to decrease mercury toxicity

Completed two years of general biology, including one college-level course

Completed two semesters of marine biology, including one college-level course

Complete one college-level course in scientific research methods.

Completed one college-level course in fisheries science.

Communications Background

Wrote report on fisheries management problems in Hawaii, presented at Science '97.

Completed four years of writing, including college-level course in technical writing.

Member, Kaimuki High School Forensics Club; presented several prepared speeches.

Winner, Honolulu Toastmasters Honorable Mention for presentation on science careers for women.

REFERENCES AVAILABLE

Sandra G. Naylor
1415 NE San Rafael Street
Santa Cruz, California 95061
Telephone: 805-555-0439

EDUCATION

1995-present   Santa Cruz Senior High School

1985-1991   Alvore School of Dance, San Francisco

EXPERIENCE

Part-time receptionist, Dr. Jonathan Naylor, Santa Cruz, 1995-present

Duties include answering telephones, calling patients to remind them about appointments, scheduling appointments, checking patients in, assisting with billing to insurance companies and patients, word processing, and filing.

SKILLS

Experienced with office reception desk responsibilities.
Computer word processing speed of 75 w.p.m.
Knowledge of WordPerfect and Quicken
Shorthand speed of 90 w.p.m.
Experienced with mail merge capabilities of computer word processing.
Pleasant telephone manner.

ACTIVITIES

Chair, Winterfest Committee
Member, Homecoming Committee
Dance team
School musicals and plays
Softball team

REFERENCES

Available upon request.

Brandon Reaman

1147 N.E. 160th   Telephone: 503-555-1361
Portland, Oregon 97230

Objective

Summer employment with construction crew.

Experience and Skills

My work experience includes assisting with roofing, building fences, and providing lawn and garden maintenance. I have worked for a private contractor to build a deck, remodel a kitchen, and reconstruct an 18 x 24-foot porch that had collapsed.

In a design and technology program, I worked with a team of three other students to design and build a balsa wood bridge that could support at least 50 pounds. Our design exceeded 100.

Able to operate the following: lathe, table saw, drill press, compression hammer, and other metal and woodworking machinery.

Work History

Crew member, Red Hat Remodeling, June-September 1997.

Crew member, Johnson Construction, June-September 1996.

Education

Reynolds High School, 1698 S.W. Cherry Park Road, Troutdale, Oregon 97060
Expected graduation date: 1993

Relevant Coursework

Practical Physics, Woods II, Metals II, Building Construction, Design and Technology

References

Available upon request

SHARON ANNE GILBERT
1735 N.E. Moore
Chattanooga, Tennessee 37402
Telephone: 615/555-3374

EDUCATION

Howard High School, 2500 Market Street, Chattanooga
Graduation date: 1999. Major: Business.

SKILLS

Word processing, filing, organizing. Able to operate the following: IBM and Macintosh computers (various word processing programs), ten-key adding machine, postage meter. Have valid driver's license.

WORK EXPERIENCE

Child care provider. Mrs. Jolie Chappell (full-time, summers) and various other families (part-time, throughout the year). 1994-present.

Provide care for children of various ages. Responsible for feeding and observing nap time and bedtime routines. I am always careful to leave the house as I found it and to help the children gain a sense of responsibility about their environment.

ACTIVITIES

Church choir and youth group
Howard High Concert Choir
Social Committee (Student Government)
One year Symphony Orchestra

REFERENCES

Available on request.

STEPHEN P. DILLON
18445 S.W. Mirick Road
Denton, Texas 76201
817-555-4550

JOB OBJECTIVE

To secure a position on a carpentry crew for full-time summer employment.

EDUCATION

Denton Senior High School, 1007 Fulton Street, Denton
Graduation date: 1999

Related courses of study: Home Building Construction (PGE Good Sense Home), Woodshop I and II, Auto Technology. Maintained top grades in each of these courses.

WORK EXPERIENCE

Worker for Buzz Burton (private contractor), August 1997-present, as work is available.
Completed deck construction project, washed and painted interior and exterior of buildings, built foundation forms. Assisted with framing and roofing.

Andersen Construction, September 1997.
Stripped and refitted a kitchen according to code specifications; installed insulation; removed and replanted shrubbery.

Excavation Crew Member, Mose Brothers Concrete, summers of 1996 and 1997.
Worked on ditch-digging crew. Operated chain saw, jumping jack, trencher, backhoe, cat loader, and dump truck.

ACTIVITIES

Four years of wrestling, two years of football, assistant coach for girls' softball.

References available upon request.

RAYMOND KELLER
1701 S. 29th Street
Sheboygan, Wisconsin 53082
Telephone: 414-555-1665

OBJECTIVE

Obtain position as apprentice mechanic in auto repair center.

EDUCATION

North High School, Sheboygan, Wisconsin 53081
Expected graduation date: 1999

COURSES TAKEN

Auto Mechanics 1-2
Career Mechanics
Principles of Technology
Metal Shop
Wood Shop
Design & Technology
Drafting
Electricity/Electronics

WORK EXPERIENCE

Shop Steward, Sheboygan North Auto Shop, 1997-present
(Student-run auto center located at high school; run diagnostics,
estimate costs, supervise repairs.)

Station Attendant, Winnebago Garage, August 1996-present

Station Attendant, Four Towers Shell, 1995-1996

ACTIVITIES

Four years high school football, Letterman's Club, boating and fishing

References are available on request.

JERIANNE JONES
1288 N.W. 58th Street
Seattle, Washington 98117
Telephone: 206/555-1941

EDUCATION

Ballard High School. Expected graduation date: 1999.

Lakeside Upper School, Seattle. Attended 1995-1997.

EXPERIENCE

Clerical: During the school year, I work in the school's central office as a clerical assistant. My responsibilities include typing, operating various duplication machines for the teachers and secretaries, filing, and delivering messages. I have received high reviews for each of the two years I have served as an assistant.

Counseling: In May 1996 and April 1997, I served as a counselor at the Bainbridge Island Outdoor School. I supervised the children on the buses and took them on discovery walks through the rain forest.

In the summers of 1995 and 1996, I spent several weeks as a YMCA camp counselor, teaching outdoor survival skills, canoeing, and swimming. I hold an up-to-date advanced lifesaving certificate.

Volunteer: As a member of the student welfare committee, I planned a social awareness week that brought speakers from several Seattle social service agencies to speak at the high school. I organized a food and clothing drive at Ballard High School for relief following earthquakes in Nicaragua and worked with a charitable organization to raise money for Romanian orphans.

ACHIEVEMENTS

Selected to present student essay on volunteerism at Lyons Club, Ballard Chapter.
Worked on student yearbook staff as copy editor.
Member of Associated Students of Ballard High School student welfare committee.

REFERENCES

Available upon request.

JORY AHRENS

131 - 172nd Avenue N.E.

Bellevue, Washington 98006

Telephone: (206) 555-9027

OBJECTIVE

To obtain a retail sales position in women's clothing department or boutique. My long-range objective is a career in fashion merchandising.

EDUCATION

Sammamish High School, 469 - 148th Avenue S.W., Bellevue
Expected graduation date: 1999

WORK EXPERIENCE

Student Manager   SHS Athletics Shop, Sammamish High School, 1997 to 1998. Worked with committee to select and purchase merchandise for student-run sports shop, which carries T-shirts and sweat-shirts, rental equipment, and sporting goods. Supervised student workers, applied transfer designs to clothing, and oversaw budgeting and finance committee.

Sales
Representative   Earrings Galore, Mall 205, 1994 to 1997. Served customers, made sales, and operated the cash register. I also assisted with preparing window displays.

SKILLS

Experienced with operating a cash register, Macintosh computer, scientific calculator, and ten-key adding machine.

ACTIVITIES

Served as a counselor at Outdoor School. Member of International Club. Played three years of team volleyball. Work at school track meets.

REFERENCES

Available upon request.

JAMES JACKSON
4217 E. Washington Street
St. Louis, MO 63119
314-555-9487

Summary

Qualified for skilled carpentry position. Experienced in rough and finished carpentry, woodworking, furniture design and construction.

Education

- Graduate, Local 7, International Carpenter's Union Apprenticeship Program
- Graduate, Lincoln Vocational High School, St. Louis, June 1998

Job Experience

1997-present   Draftsman, Belle Architectural Inc.   St. Louis

Responsible for drafting and blueprint reading, construction of scale models for architects.

1994-1997   Assistant Manager, Blair Woodworking   St. Louis

Assisted owner of precision woodworking shop with design and production of custom furniture. Special-order projects for home owners and builders.

References

Business and personal references on request. Detailed photo portfolio available.

Nicholas Vittaco
822 Hillside Drive
Brooklyn, New York 10036
212-555-8756

GOAL   *Entry-level job as drafter for a local architectural firm.*

TRAINING   *Graduate, McMurray Technical High School*
             June 1998

HONORS   *Voted Outstanding Senior by teachers and classmates*

             Maintained G.P.A. of 3.5/Honor Roll Status

WORK
HISTORY   *Construction Worker, Benson & Sons, Brooklyn, New York*
             Summers, 1994 to 1998

             *Worked summer construction jobs throughout high school.
             *Operated heavy equipment.
             *Delivered building materials to job sites.
             *Achieved rank of junior carpenter.

             ~References will be provided upon request~

Marilyn Smith
418 Whitesburn Street
Wauconda, IL 60084
847-555-9822

Objective   Nurse Assistant Position

Employment

1997-present   **Nurse Assistant, Pinkerton Nursing Center, Wauconda, IL**

Give report to RNs regarding status of patients and current needs. Assist patients with bathing, grooming needs. Monitor and record fluid intake and output, vital signs, general changes in mood or appearance. Promote mental and physical health of patients while assisting nursing staff.

1995-1997   **Office Assistant, Kusler Medical Group, Deerfield, IL**

Maintained patient files, answered phones, scheduled appointments, typed correspondence. Provided general clerical support for busy pediatric office.

Education   Nursing Assistant Certification
Columbia Vocational Institute, Chicago, IL
June 1997

Graduate
Wauconda High School, Wauconda, IL
June 1995

References   Available on request

Chapter Six

SAMPLE COVER LETTERS

Juan Aguilar

~ 158 Halliday S.W. ~ Benton Harbor, MI 49028 ~ (616) 555-7379 ~

September 1, 19--

Mr. Charles Hensen
Production Manager
The Herald-Palladium
3450 Hollywood Road
St. Joseph, MI 49085

Dear Mr. Hensen:

Mr. George Petersen of Michigan Printing suggested I contact you with regard to my enthusiastic interest in a career in the printing industry. I would like to apply for a position as an apprentice printer and have enclosed my resume for your consideration.

This past summer I worked for Mr. Petersen as a print shop assistant. As the summer vacation relief worker, I was able to move throughout the printing department, and in the process I learned a tremendous amount about the trade. In addition, my course work in graphic arts and computer applications has given me a background that will be very useful in mastering electronic pre-press techniques.

I would very much appreciate an opportunity to come by to talk with you and see the printing operations at the newspaper. Mr. Petersen spoke very highly of the production department, and I hope to become part of your team. I will call you within the next few days, or you may reach me at the above number most afternoons.

Sincerely,

Juan Aguilar

September 20, 19--

Mr. Henry B. Thurston
Assistant to the Director
Washington Children's Services Division
220 W. First
Seattle, WA 98022

Dear Mr. Thurston:

I am writing to apply for an internship with the Washington Children's Services Division. I understand from my child development instructor, Susan Bishop, that you have four such positions available each summer.

My educational training in child development and psychology has already been beneficial in programs I have been involved with. I have become especially interested in carrying anti-drug and alcohol messages to young people. Toward this end, I worked with the Boys and Girls Club of South Seattle and started a club at Tyee High School, "Tyee (Naturally) High Club," which has stirred a tremendous response among students.

I will be happy to serve CSD in whatever capacity I may be most useful. I have a variety of skills in addition to those listed on my resume. Specifically, I am familiar with computer word processing and am quite skilled at general clerical work. I would like to speak with you at your convenience about your expectations for the student intern and how I might best contribute to CSD's efforts. My telephone number is 555-9225, and I am generally at home in the early morning and late afternoon.

Sincerely,

Jason Raintree
2268-A South 187th Street
Seattle, WA 98055

2250 Collis Avenue
Huntington, WV 25702

June 26, 19--

Mr. Frank Westerman
Fire Chief
Huntington Fire District
680 Temple Avenue
Huntington, WV 25702

Dear Mr. Westerman:

I was delighted to see your advertisement for firefighter trainees in yesterday's *Herald Dispatch* because it has been my lifelong ambition to become a firefighter. My resume is enclosed for your review.

My activities and course work in high school have centered on health, physical fitness, and sports. I have maintained excellent physical condition, which your advertisement indicates is a must for prospective firefighters. I have also had advanced training in first aid and CPR.

Once you have had an opportunity to review my resume, I will call to set up an appointment at your convenience to further discuss my interests and qualifications. I am eager to pursue a career in fire prevention and protection.

Sincerely,

Robert Goldstein
304-555-6938

May 15, 19--

J. E. Davis
Stanton Electronics
2516 West Palm Drive, Suite 116
Laguna Beach, CA 92653

Dear J. E. Davis:

In reply to your recent advertisement in the *Times*, I have enclosed my resume for consideration in your search for an electronics technician.

I believe my training and experience provide me with the background you are looking for. My work in the design and manufacturing of radar-controlled devices will allow me to immediately take on the challenges of Stanton Electronics.

I look forward to having an opportunity to visit your facilities and talk with you about the projects I have completed. I will be happy to bring some of the more relevant of these in order for you to see the quality of my work and the innovation in the designs. My number is (213) 555-9562, and I may be reached most mornings.

Thank you for your consideration.

Sincerely,

Masoud Ysmiri
211 South Grevillea Avenue
Apt. 26B
Inglewood, CA 90301

3836 Sweetwater Avenue
Scottsdale, AZ 85254

May 6, 19--

Carol Emory
Emory & Associates
One West Monroe
Suite 2017
Phoenix, AZ 85004

Dear Ms. Emory:

I am writing to request the opportunity to work for you as a summer intern. I understand from my adviser at Stanford that your firm often takes on summer interns.

I will graduate from Chaparral High School in Scottsdale this month and will enter Stanford's pre-law program in September. I hope to use my summer to learn more about private legal practice by working in whatever way I might best contribute to your firm.

As the enclosed resume indicates, I am a hard worker who takes pride in doing the best possible job at every task I take on. I hold a 4.0 grade point average and will graduate in the top five percent of my class. I have experience in clerical work, and I am willing to put in the long hours that are standard for anyone involved in legal practice.

I would like to arrange a time to visit with you at your convenience to learn more about how I can contribute my abilities. My telephone number is (602) 555-2834, and I am available after 3:30 daily.

Yours sincerely,

Paul Garcia

435 South Monaco Parkway
Denver, CO 80204
February 15, 19--

Mr. John Seward
Seward and Whitely, CPAs
21 West Riddlington
Denver, CO 80216

Dear Mr. Seward:

I am responding to the February 10 advertisement in the *Post* announcing openings for part-time temporary accounting clerks. My resume is enclosed for your review.

As my resume indicates, I have received extensive training in accounting and bookkeeping and am familiar with several computer software programs that deal with accounting. Working for your company would be a timely opportunity to put these skills to the challenge of aiding your firm during the tax season. Upon graduation, I hope to pursue a college degree in accounting.

I would appreciate an opportunity to meet with you, at your convenience, to discuss the position. The advertisement indicated that hours were flexible, and as I am still in school, I would be available to work any day after 2:00 p.m. and could extend my hours as long as necessary to accomplish the job. I may be reached at 555-4481 any afternoon.

Thank you for your consideration. I look forward to talking with you.

Sincerely,

Michael Han

128 Orange Street
New Haven, CT 06510

April 26, 19--

Ms. Verna Howard, Office Manager
Benson, Keller, Harcourt, and Vinson, Attorneys at Law
12 Front Avenue, Suite 1200
New Haven, CT 06508

Dear Ms. Howard:

I am enclosing a resume and letters of recommendation, submitted in response to your advertisement for a paralegal assistant that appeared in the April 20th *New Haven Gazette.*

I will graduate with highest honors from Hillhouse High School next month following a four-year curriculum centered on business, law, and office management. I believe my training and my previous experience as an office assistant for the firm of Switter, Harvey, Jenkins & Hewitt have prepared me for assuming the responsibilities of a paralegal assistant.

I would appreciate the opportunity to meet with you at your convenience. I am eager to put my skills to work for your firm. I may be reached at 555-3754 in the afternoons.

Thank you for considering my application.

Yours truly,

Judy Reimer

2240 Nebraska Avenue N.W.
Washington, D.C. 20016

May 28, 19--

Ms. Belinda Summers
Director
Jefferson Montessori School
620 Jefferson Avenue N.W.
Washington, D.C. 20018

Dear Ms. Summers:

I would like to put forward my application for a summer program guide position at Jefferson Montessori, advertised in Sunday's *City Herald*.

I was a Montessori child myself, through the eighth grade, and am both familiar with and appreciative of the program's philosophy. My experiences as a day camp leader and outdoor school counselor have firmed my resolve to enter a career in early childhood education. I believe my background in Montessori as well as my training and experiences in working with children enable me to make a worthwhile contribution to your school.

In addition, as a Native American, I have taken special efforts to learn the history, crafts, songs, and dances of my heritage. By teaching songs, stories, and crafts, I am able to share with others the richness of my native culture. I have had experience directing such activities with children of various ages.

I would like to visit the school and talk with you at your convenience. I am available any afternoon and can be reached at 555-7465. Thank you for your consideration; I look forward to meeting you.

Sincerely,

Mary Jo Baptiste

990 Woody Road
Dallas, Texas 75253

15 May 19--

Anita Blakeley, Manager
Blakeley Distributors
886 Denton Road
Dallas, Texas 75259

Dear Ms. Blakeley:

I would like to apply for the position of assistant manager advertised in the May 9 edition of the *Times Herald.*

As indicated in the enclosed resume, I have had some previous managerial experience. At Taco Time my duties frequently included taking over full responsibility for restaurant operations in the absence of the manager. I became adept at dealing with a variety of crises, from finding substitutes for workers who failed to report to work during rush hour to dealing successfully with surprise inspections from the health and fire departments.

As a recent high school graduate, I may seem young, but I would like to emphasize my commitment to a long-term relationship with Blakeley Distributors. I would like to use my organizational skills, business training, and interpersonal skills to serve your company to the best of my ability.

I hope to have an opportunity to talk with you at your convenience about my experiences and training and how they qualify me for the job. My telephone number is 555-2369, and I am available most mornings.

Thank you for your consideration.

Sincerely,

Brian McGavin

Kendra Wallen

1137 N.E. 189th ~ Provo, Utah ~ (801) 55-2740

March 11, 19--

Sandra Mason
Director
YMCA Lakeside Camp
22 Lakshore Road
Provo, Utah 84612

Dear Ms. Mason:

I would like to submit my resume for your consideration in selecting teachers for this summer's camp programs. Having attended camp as an elementary school student for several years, I am familiar with the program and believe I have a lot to contribute toward making the summer camp experience memorable for others.

My concentration in high school has been art, and I have used my training and love of all art media to develop projects that would be fun and rewarding for children, from preschool age through sixth grade. Projects have included paper and fabric marbling, tie-dying T-shirts, making pottery beads, and making natural dyes from leaves, roots, and other items gathered on nature walks.

I would like to show you the results of some of these projects and further discuss my qualifications with you. Please call me at your convenience. I can be reached at the number above in the afternoons, or you may leave and message and I will return your call promptly. Thank you very much for considering my application.

Yours truly,

Kendra Wallen

Claire Renard

618 N.W. Eighth Street, No. 215
Boca Raton, Florida 33486
Telephone: 941-555-1400

May 12, 19--

Mr. Harold Washington
Assistant Manager
Florida State Bank
224 N.W. Fifth Street
Boca Raton, FL 33486

Dear Mr. Washington:

I am writing in response to your advertisement for bank tellers that appeared in the *Times* on May 6. My resume and two letters of recommendation are enclosed, as requested.

As indicated in my resume, the focus of my course work has been business and accounting. My experiences as treasurer of the student body and on the school's student finance committee have provided an excellent opportunity for me to exercise the skills learned in the classroom. I was responsible for managing the budget for the entire student body, authorizing disbursements, developing a financial plan for the year, and providing monthly financial reports.

I would like to arrange an interview at your convenience so that I may learn more about your expectations for prospective tellers. I believe I can assure you that I will meet your qualifications. I may be reached at the above number in the afternoons and any time after May 21st.

Thank you for your consideration.

Yours truly,

Claire Renard

Laura Chen
5527 N.W. Oak Creek Road
Ashland, Oregon 97520
(503) 555-9882

May 18, 19--

Mr. Everard Carlisle, Director
Sierra Club International, Central Office
358 Geary
San Francisco, CA 94101

Dear Mr. Carlisle:

The position announced in the May 2 *Chronicle* appears to be the perfect opportunity to put
my skills in science and business, together with my abiding interest in the environment, to work
for the betterment of the earth. I am enclosing my resume in application for the entry-level position
in your research and economics division.

As my resume indicates, I have an extensive background in the earth and natural sciences, as well
as a strong record in business and economics courses. Capstone economics, in particular, was a
challenging course that allowed students the opportunity to unravel economic mysteries by
learning and practicing careful economic reasoning in analysis of particular economic situations.
I chose as my topic of endeavor to anticipate and evaluate the impact of the balanced budget
amendment on federal environmental programs. It was a fascinating project, and I would enjoy
having the opportunity to share the findings with you.

I am planning a trip to the Bay Area early next month and would like to visit with you at that time,
if possible. The dates of my trip are not yet settled, so I can arrange my schedule to your convenience.
Please write to me at the above address, or call me at (503) 555-9982. I look forward to speaking
with you.

Sincerely,

Laura Chen

May 26, 19--

Ms. Elaine Richardson
Personnel Director
Microsoft Corporation
226 Industrial Parkway
Everett, WA 98203

Dear Ms. Richardson:

I would like to submit my resume in application for an entry-level position in the research and development department. I will be attending the University of Washington in Seattle this fall in computer programming, and I believe my experience and training thus far will enable me to be an asset to Microsoft.

My high school computer teacher, Mr. Earl Phillips, is a gifted computer scientist, and it has been a great privilege to study with him. He has challenged my own innate interest and ability in computer programming and technology to push my ideas toward greater and greater innovation. I have tackled programming problems in BASIC, PASCAL, FORTRAN, and Hypercard environments, working on DOS, Macintosh, and UNIX platforms.

I would appreciate an opportunity to meet with you and the director of research and development and share the results of my own programming efforts. I will be moving to the Seattle area within the next week and will contact you shortly thereafter. I look forward to seeing the Microsoft operation firsthand.

Thank you for your consideration.

Sincerely,

Dylan J. McDonald
1415 Wenig Road N.E.
Cedar Rapids, IA 52402

2248 W. Billtown Road, Apt. 16
Louisville, KY 40215
Telephone: 502/555-7751

June 3, 19--

Ms. Theresa Valdez
Staff Nurse
Louisville Care Center
16815 W. MacKay
Louisville, KY 40215

Dear Ms. Valdez:

I would like to submit my resume to you in application for a position as a nurse's
aide at the Louisville Care Center. I spoke with your assistant, Jenna Bradley,
who indicated that there were two such positions available and that I should
write to you directly.

My experiences as a candy striper at Louisville General have made me aware that
working in a health care facility is often very tough, both physically and emotionally.
I believe, however, that I am equal to the challenge, and I would very much like to make
a contribution to the success of Louisville Care Center.

I would like to come in and speak with you about my qualifications and how I can
best fulfill your expectations for this position. I look forward to hearing from you.
I am available at the above number most mornings. Thank you for your consideration.

Yours truly,

SUZANNE BARSTOW

May 22, 19--

Mr. Bradford Williamson
Personnel Director
Electronics Enterprises
1810 S. Olive
Los Angeles, California 90015

Dear Mr. Williamson:

I am writing to reply to your advertisement in the Sunday *Times* for technicians. Please accept my resume in application for the position.

I have two years of classroom training in design and technology, a program designed to allow students to define and solve their own technological design problems. I have also had course work in electronics, engine mechanics, and computer-assisted drafting. Two of the projects I developed in these courses (a solar-powered car and a computer-directed light and sound presentation) have been submitted to national competition.

I would appreciate receiving an opportunity to meet with you and discuss my qualifications for the position of technician. I may be reached at (213) 555-9226 in the afternoons and will arrange to meet at your convenience. Thank you for considering my application.

Sincerely yours,

Toby Waterson
200 South Third Avenue
Arcadia, CA 91006

3320 Delaware Avenue
Buffalo, New York 14222

May 12, 19--

Ms. Susan Simonson, Manager
Musicland
128 North Seventh Avenue
Buffalo, New York 14225

Dear Ms. Simonson:

In reply to your advertisement in the *Buffalo News* of May 16, I am enclosing my resume
to apply for the position of evening salesclerk.

I have had a serious interest in music for many years, and have received formal training
in both classical and jazz singing. My listening interests in music are much broader,
and I keep up-to-date on contemporary musicians from rap to rock.

I would like to set up a time at your convenience to visit the store and talk with you
about the position. I am currently working as a singing hostess, but would enjoy the
opportunity to work in retail sales for a company involved with music. I can be reached
at 555-2193 after 3:30 most afternoons.

Thank you for the opportunity to apply.

Sincerely,

Michelle M. Hibbard

412 Lincoln
Las Vegas, NV 87701

May 22, 19--

Mr. Eric Swenson
Personnel Director
The Mirage
One Mirage Court
Las Vegas, NV 87702

Dear Mr. Swenson:

I am writing to apply for a position with one of The Mirage's restaurants. I am interested in serving as a waiter, busboy, or kitchen assistant. John Rivers at Circus Circus suggested I write to you concerning the availability of summer employment.

I worked for Mr. Rivers last summer, and though he was pleased with my work, I would prefer to gain more experience in the restaurant area of hotel operations. I am currently working at Denny's, but am eager to return to a hotel environment. I plan to continue my education in hotel and restaurant management.

I would appreciate an opportunity to talk with you about summer employment opportunities at The Mirage. I have long admired the hotel and would enjoy doing my best to serve your restaurant guests. Please call me at 555-6623 at your convenience.

Thank you for your consideration.

Sincerely,

Paul Jerome

2240 W. Yucca Street
Santa Fe, New Mexico 87538

May 20, 19--

Personnel Director
Bellande Enterprises Inc.
305 E. 102nd
Santa Fe, New Mexico 87536

Dear Director:

Today my accounting teacher, Ms. Cheryl Cooper, informed the class about several local job openings in the business field. The secretarial position with your company got my immediate attention. I would like to apply for this opening and have enclosed my resume for your consideration.

I have held two summer secretarial positions, both of which provided me with excellent clerical experience. My tasks included word processing, managing a six-line switchboard, and operating a ten-key adding machine, as well as light bookkeeping and data entry. My specialized courses in business operations and accounting have given me the specific skills needed to take on the challenges of a secretarial position. I am very responsible and organized, and I believe I will be an asset to your company.

Thank you for taking the time to review my resume. I would enjoy working for Bellande and would appreciate an opportunity to talk with you at your convenience. I may be reached after 3:00 at 555-5121.

Sincerely,

Maruya Angelino

Shelley Tabor

78 N.E. Towbridge
Bridgewater, MA 02324

May 26, 19--

Ms. Paula Marshall
Director
Little Wonder Day Care
26 W. Fifth Avenue
Bridgewater, MA 02326

Dear Ms. Marshall:

I am writing in response to your advertisement in this week's *Bridgewater Times* for
a part-time teaching assistant at Little Wonder Day Care. My resume is enclosed
for your consideration.

I have been involved with young children for as long as I can remember. I have four
younger siblings, ranging in age from three to fifteen. As the eldest, I was often
responsible for watching over them.

For the past five years, I have provided child care for two families, including two summers
of full-time care for three children. I always work hard at maintaining a happy, supportive
environment, often bringing books and various art or music projects to share with the
children. I never rely on television as a substitute for supervision.

I have received formal training in childhood development and education from school
courses and experience with the in-school day care center/preschool. The Preschool
Practicum, one semester working half-days in the day care center, was an exceptional
experience that convinced me to pursue a career in early childhood education.

I would like to come and talk with you further about the position and my qualifications.
I am available most mornings at 555-8281. Thank you for considering how I might
assist the staff at Little Wonder.

Sincerely,

Shelley Tabor